DATE DUE

GAYLORD			PRINTED IN U.S.A.

ROSS PEROT:
Businessman Politician

Notable Americans

ROSS PEROT:
Businessman Politician

Aaron Boyd
and
Michael Causey

Greensboro

ROSS PEROT: *Businessman Politician*

Copyright © 1994 by Aaron Boyd and Michael Causey

Library of Congress Cataloging-in-Publication Data
Boyd, Aaron, 1955-
  Ross Perot: businessman politician / Aaron Boyd and Michael Causey.
     p. cm. -- (Notable Americans)
  Includes bibliographical references and index.
  ISBN 1-883846-04-8
  1. Perot, H. Ross, 1930- --Juvenile literature.   2. Presidential
candidates--United States--Biography--Juvenile literature.
3. Businessmen--United States--Biography--Juvenile literature.
[1. Perot, H. Ross, 1930-   . 2. Presidential candidates.
3. Businessmen.]   I. Causey, Michael, 1947- .   II. Title.
III. Series.
E840.8. P427B69   1994
973.928' 092 -- dc20
[B]
                                                       93-33189
                                                          CIP
                                                           AC

Printed in the United States of America

First Edition

5 4 3 2 1

To
Our Mothers

CONTENTS

BOY FROM TEXARKANA

Ross Perot, the man who would become one of the world's wealthiest men, a business legend in the world of business and finance, a folk hero to millions of Americans, was not born to wealth and privilege. He was born Henry Ray Perot, the second son of Lulu May and Gabriel Ross Perot in Texarkana, Texas, on June 27, 1930. The middle name Ross was later added as a tribute to a brother, Gabriel Ross Jr., who had died of spinal meningitis before Henry Ray was born.

Texarkana, and the East Texas region along the Arkansas border where it is located, have much to do with the values and habits Ross learned as a young boy and adolescent, and have much to do with the kind of man he is today.

The area around Texarkana was settled in the decades after 1800, largely by Scotch-Irish homesteaders, pioneers by the standards of that day. Many of them or their parents had settled first in the Carolinas, or in Georgia, Alabama, or Mississippi. But, as the slave and plantation economy began to flourish in the South, many had lost their land to unscrupulous land speculators or dishonest bankers and politicians. So they kept moving, searching for a place to live a simple life in rugged freedom, until they came to East Texas, a land that very few people wanted. Here they put down roots, grubbed and scratched a living from the land, and made a community where people shared the same simple and sometimes hard-bitten values.

Ross Perot's great-grandfather was just such an immigrant. A small merchant and fur trader of French descent, he moved from Louisiana to the area around Texarkana in the middle 1800s and began a general store. His son and later his grandson (G. R. Perot, Ross's father) followed in his footsteps, building up the store and later expanding into the cotton wholesaling business.

G.R. Perot took a detour, however. When he was fourteen, his father died and, not yet old enough to run a business, he spent several years as a cowboy, herding cattle and mending fences as a hired man. By 1918, however, just as the First World War ended, he was back in the business of buying and selling cotton, and put up a sign over his business that stated his needs in a down-home way.

G.R. Perot
Cotton Buyer
Sell it, you can't eat it

By 1923, he had met and married Lulu Mae Ray, who worked as a secretary for a lumber company. The couple built a home at 2901 Olive Street and began to raise a family. Illness took their first child, but a daughter, Bette, was born soon after. Doctors had warned Lulu Mae that she should not have any more children, but she was determined, and on one of the hottest days ever recorded in that hot part of the country, Ross was born.

By all accounts, the Perot household was a loving one. G.R., a heavy man who was barely five feet tall, had much affection and respect for his wife. Bette remembers that the couple often held hands, and enjoyed going to dances, a favorite activity of the rotund but graceful G.R., at a place called the Club Lido.

Though later to be known internationally as "H. Ross",

Perot was never called that by family or friends. "Never once in my life have I referred to myself as H. Ross Perot," he has stated, saying that name sounded "ostentatious." Ross, who was called "Brother" at home, learned many of his values from his father and mother. First and foremost was that he and his sister Bette were to obey their parents, to be polite to their elders, to deal honestly with other people and to be good neighbors. "I grew up in a home where you were expected to do what you were supposed to do," Ross says simply.

The elder Perots were people of simple tastes. They did not believe in borrowing money or being in debt. The one exception was the house on Olive Street, which Mr. Perot had borrowed about 4400 dollars to buy—but that loan was paid back within a year.

Ross had great respect for, and was close to, his father, a family man who came home to eat lunch with the family and who spent much time with the children. The elder Perot was a horse fancier who put up a small stable on a vacant lot across the street from the home. The family owned several horses on which Ross or his sister Bette would go for rides with their father. It was during this time, Ross would say later, that he learned many life lessons from his father. "My dad was my closest friend and he gave me a lot of time."

As a youngster of eight, Ross earned money "breaking" horses — taking an animal and taming it. He was paid $1.00 a piece for the work. Although the horse-breaking was profitable, it was also a bruising experience. Ross suffered several hard knocks on the head and broke his nose, along with bruised ribs and a sore backside. But then he decided to work smarter, not harder. He devised a method of tying up one of the horse's front legs under the animal with a cloth cinch. This did not hurt the animal, but as horses have a fear of losing their balance and falling, the animal became hesitant and less aggressive. Ross was then able to mount the horse and quickly establish who was boss. He was able to train more horses and make more money with this ingenious method.

The young Perot used a horse in another inventive way to earn spending money. Like many youngsters in those days, Ross wanted to get a job as a paper boy, delivering the *Texarkana Gazette*. The only available route was one through a very poor district of town, a rough and sometimes dangerous area called New Town, where there were houses of prostitution and "flop houses" (rooming houses for transient men and hobos).

Ross seemed to be an easy target for the occasional man who, on a Sunday morning after a drunken Saturday night, tried to take the paper boy's bag of coins collected as his week's wages. Occasionally, someone tried to steal his money; but the horse was big and fast, and Ross simply rode away to safety.

Because no one else had worked the route, Ross had asked for special payment terms from the newspaper. "I was making 25 to 30 dollars a week. The newspaper thought that was too much so they tried to change my rate to what the other carriers were getting." Ross then says he decided to go to the paper's publisher, a Mr. Palmer. As he would later do in more public and national debates, Ross made a direct appeal. Mr. Palmer agreed with Ross, and the rate change was not put into place. "Since then, whenever I've got a problem, I always go to the top," Ross says.

In that day and time, children were expected to help out with family finances if they could, and Ross took to this duty with a dash of the businessman he would later become. By the age of eight or nine, he was earning a few extra dollars by selling things door to door around the residential areas in Texarkana. He rang doorbells and sold subscriptions to magazines such as *The Saturday Evening Post.* In the spring he sold vegetable seeds for the many home gardens people had then. In the winter he sold Christmas cards for the upcoming holiday season. And, though it was unusual for someone so young, he took on a job as a debt collector, riding his bicycle all over town to collect small sums of money from people who had run classified ads in the newspaper.

Young Ross's determination and struggle to save a few dollars was not very different from the prevailing attitudes of the town. It was not unusual for a drought to ruin crops in the field, a tornado to swoop down and wreak havoc, or a flood to wipe out a family's life savings. But the people would rebuild, and continue on. Ross later referred to this attitude as a "tough optimism." He remembers as a youngster "seeing the Red River come over its banks and wash away houses, barns, crops, everything. And the men just standing there like pieces of rock . . . The water'd go down, you'd rebuild it and hope it'd be a few years before it would happen again."

Texarkana was a rail center, and many freight trains came through from all parts of the country. In the late 1930's, when Ross was still a small boy, The Great Depression still gripped the country. Many men who were out of work "rode the rails," as hobos or "bums," some trying to find work, some simply trying to stay alive. Quite a few of these men, hungry and homeless, seemed to turn up at the Perot's back door, and asked if they could do odd jobs in exchange for something to eat. Lulu Perot was always willing to fix a plate of food or a sandwich for the hobos.

One day a tramp told Mrs. Perot why so many homeless vagabonds showed up at her house. As Ross remembers, "He showed her where the tramps had made a mark on the curb in front of our house. That was a sign to other tramps that they would be fed there. After the man left, I said, 'Mother, do you want me to wipe that off?' And she said, 'No, leave it there. Those people are just like you and me. The difference is, they're down on their luck.'"

The elder Perots believed strongly that education was the key to success in life. G.R. Perot had had to quit school because his father died; Lulu May was proud that she had been able to get a high school diploma before going to work.

The couple wanted the best for their children. The closest thing to a private school in Texarkana was called the Patty Hill School, operated out of the home of the teacher, Mrs. Mary C. Patterson. Both Bette and Ross were enrolled there, at 15 dollars a month tuition, which was serious money during the last years of the Depression.

The school, however, lived up to its reputation as a place where children were encouraged to express themselves in artistic ways as well as through academics. Students were schooled in literature and art, and several times a year the grammar school class produced and performed a play or other recital in public, for parents and other townspeople. (Ross, never a gifted musician, tried unsuccessfully to learn the accordion for one show.) Apart from this liberal curriculum, however, the students were expected to learn Latin and to memorize passages from the Bible for daily recitation. Discipline was tough. Students could expect a hard rap on the knuckles with a ruler if they had not learned the day's lessons, or for acting up in class.

But, when Ross transferred to public school in the fifth grade, he had a solid foundation of learning with a good, if not spectacular, grade average. And perhaps more importantly, he had the experience of performing and speaking to an audience. Fred Graham, former Law Correspondent for CBS News, was also a student at Patty Hill School. He says, "There's not much stage fright among the graduates of Patty Hill."

Attendance at the local Methodist Church was a weekly ritual in the family. Lulu Perot was active as a volunteer in the church, and with the Boy Scouts and other youth groups. It was not long before Ross joined local Troop #18, and at age 12 showed what might have been the first evidence in his young life of the will to high achievement.

Only about one out of every hundred Scouts makes it to the rank of Eagle Scout, the highest award in Scouting; it usually takes four or five years for a teenager to complete all the merit badges and tests of skills necessary to earn this highest ranking. Ross made Eagle Scout in 16 months.

Ross was greatly influenced by the local scoutmaster, Sam Shuman, a Lithuanian Jew who, as an immigrant recently arrived in the United States, was perhaps even more patriotic and a bigger believer in the American Dream than the flag-waving Texarkanans. Shuman laced his scouting tips with big doses of his own belief that, in America, hard work and a determination to succeed are the main tools needed to make it to the top.

Ross is still a big booster and benefactor of the Boy Scouts, and in one of his early acts of charity, funded a Scout center in Texarkana. There, in a glass case, he has reassembled and donated much of the memorabilia from his Scouting days: his campaign hat, a hand-crafted beaded belt he made as a Cub Scout, his merit badges and other awards. His old Boy Scout Manual is the most prominent item in the display. Its worn cover and tattered pages reveal that it had been read and studied for countless hours.

The elder Perot taught Ross lessons in business early on. The two went together to the many cattle auctions in the area, and with some guidance from his father, Ross bought and sold saddles and horse bridles, as well as farm animals.

Ross became what was known as a "day trader." The idea was to buy an animal, a horse or steer, in the morning and then sell it the same day for a small profit. "But I couldn't take anything home. If you took something home, you'd have to feed it."

G. R. Perot based much of his business on personal friendship and trust. Ross often accompanied his father during the winter, when he would make personal visits to some of his clients, the farmers who grew the cotton. Often the farmer's life was bitter and hard, and these visits helped the farmer break up the monotony and loneliness of his off-season life. Ross began to understand that his father was more than a businessman to these farmers and their families —he was a friend.

Others in the Perot clan were fiercely independent and believed that all things were possible. Uncle Henry Ray, Lulu's brother, was a favorite of the young Ross. As a young man, Henry had wanted to become a pilot. In those days, daring pilots "barnstormed" the country, performing aerial aerobatics in rickety planes of World War I vintage. These air shows were particularly popular in the Midwest and the South, where entertainment was hard to come by. However, Henry had no money to purchase a plane. As the family legend has it, Henry bought a war surplus airplane engine and, working from diagrams he found in a magazine, actually built his own small plane and learned to fly it.

Whether or not all this happened as reported, Uncle Henry did volunteer for the armed forces, and though a few years over the age limit, fought for his country throughout World War II as a solider in the Signal Corps in Burma and

China. He was a hero and role model for the young teenager, as was Perot's cousin Ross Hoffman, a bomber pilot who flew hazardous missions over Nazi Germany from bases in Great Britain.

Perhaps because of these examples, it was Ross's dream to attend the United States Naval Academy in Annapolis, Maryland. This was not an unusual wish for a young man graduating from high school only a few years after World War II. The Naval Academy, though, was also desirable because the education was free of charge. However, Annapolis was not easy to get into. In the absence of superior grades, Ross's only chance was to convince his congressman to recommend him for admission. Ross wrote several letters, but with no response. So, he decided to attend nearby Texarkana Junior College, which had a two-year course of study, and was located on the same block as Texarkana High School. It was here, in the college attended by local kids and a few returning servicemen, that Ross began to show the leadership abilities that were to make him successful as an adult.

Perot learned that the yearbook, called *The Bulldog*, had not been published since before the war. He was able to convince the college deans to provide funding for the yearbook to be published again.

Old classmates remember that Ross was a loyal friend who could be fun to be around, but that he had an almost compulsive urge to involve himself in student controversies. Once involved, he argued his point of view so strongly that it could be irritating. Also, perhaps because he had spent much of his life running and managing small enterprises such as the paper route and the "horse breaking" business, when he involved himself with a project, he felt almost compelled to try to manage it according to his ideas. Once he had taken the initiative to bring back the yearbook, it took a concerted effort on the part of the editors to pry him away from it. Ross's determination paid off in another way, however. He was elected class president in his second year at Texarkana Junior College.

However, though he could be single-minded, Perot's instincts were often correct. During his sophomore year, Ross became involved in an important campus issue, which carried over into the public arena. Along with other campus leaders, he urged the college board to move the junior college campus away from the neighboring high school to its own, much larger site. The students argued that the college had no room to expand with the community. The decision, however, went against Ross's position. But Perot would not give up. After discussing the matter with his family, he organized public support for moving the campus by visiting the Chamber of Commerce and other city officials. Though in 1948 this was considered a cheeky, almost pushy thing for a mere student to do, he made an impressive presentation.

The campaign was his first taste of fighting in the area of public affairs, and it finally was successful. Texarkana Junior College is now situated on the 90 acre site which Ross Perot argued and agitated for as a student.

Though Ross was doing well at Texarkana, and had considered attending law school at the University of Texas, he was still writing letters to his congressman, asking for a chance to attend Annapolis. His persistence finally paid off. So the story goes, Senator W. Lee "Pappy" O'Daniel of Texas was in Washington D.C., cleaning out his office to leave the capital to retire. An aide happened to mention a piece of last minute business: one appointment to Annapolis was still unfilled. The Senator asked, "Does anybody want it?" The aide, remembering the letters, mentioned "this kid from Texarkana," who seemed to want the appointment very much. "Give it to him then," said the Senator.

The "kid from Texarkana," of course, was Ross Perot.

MIDSHIPMAN PEROT

Before leaving for Annapolis, Ross decided to bum around the country. He left Texarkana for two weeks of hitchhiking down into Mexico and back again. When he returned he only had 55 cents in his pocket, but he had enjoyed himself and seen a good part of the Southwest.

Perhaps it was good that he had had this taste of freedom, for when he arrived at the Naval Academy it was to a life of strict discipline and hard work. Annapolis would be his entire life for the next four years. He was sworn in as a new cadet on his birthday on June 27, 1949.

The first year recruits were known as "plebes" by upper-classman and were subjected to various sorts of harassment, called "hazing," as an effort to instill discipline and to weed out the students who were not able to put up with the severe physical schedule and the emotional strain of life at the Academy. Cadets marched everywhere, even to the dining hall, and were expected to study at least one hour outside of class for every hour spent in class. All of this was expected to be hard, a tough process, but Ross thrived in this atmosphere.

Ross was not near the honor roll academically. "I was an average student," he remembers. "I really didn't have the background." But he did respectably well in his classes, which were mostly math and engineering courses. However, very early on he impressed both the cadets and his officers with his personality.

One of the main goals of the Naval Academy was to develop those qualities which could be called "Leadership"; and here Ross truly excelled. Perhaps due to his training at the Patty Hill School, or his debating experience at Texarkana Junior College, by the time he reached Annapolis Ross had the poise necessary to impress both his classmates and his superiors.

Ross's obvious leadership qualities and no-nonsense style made him popular and respected among the student body. As a sophomore, he was elected Vice-President of his class. As a senior, he was elected class president and named head of the Honor Committee, a student group responsible for judging and setting the punishment for students involved in breaches of the honor code. Perot took his job here quite seriously.

In one memorable case, he disagreed strongly when a student with an influential father was given a slap on the wrist for what Ross considered a serious breach of the honor code. In protest, he resigned from the Honor Committee, and went further to resign as class president as well. Annapolis authorities decided to investigate the case, and finally meted out an appropriate punishment to the student. Ross was talked into taking his place as class president, and head of the Honor Committee, once again.

Margot Birmingham was studying sociology and anthropology at Goucher College, when a friend asked her to go on a double date to a Naval Academy dance. Her blind date was to be a young man named Ross Perot.

Ross remembers it was "love at first sight," at least for him. Margot, although impressed, was not bowled over by the Annapolis student, but she definitely wanted to keep seeing him. "He was the first Texan I ever met," she recalls.

"I knew that I wanted to be around him. Life was exciting when he was there."

Ross recalls the situation slightly differently. Mutual friends later told him that, on returning to Goucher, Margot was asked about her blind date, and that she thought for a few seconds and finally said, "Well, he's very clean." She insisted later she meant that he was clean cut, with good manners. Ross never had any illusions that he was so handsome or so charming that he would sweep a pretty young woman like Margot off her feet. But he was nothing if not persistent, and in time his personality would win Margot over.

A highlight of Ross's college career would come when then-President Dwight Eisenhower and his wife Mamie stopped over at Annapolis while on a short cruise from Washington on the Presidential yacht. Ross, as senior class president, was chosen to escort the President around the campus during his visit.

In one yearbook, the following is said about Perot: "What Ross lacked in physical size, he more than adequately replaced by his capacity to win friends and influence people."

After graduation in 1953, Ross reported aboard the *USS Sigourney* for an around-the-world cruise, the first of his four years of obligatory military service.

It was a plum assignment. The *Sigourney* was a destroyer, one of the smaller ships in the Navy, and a place where a young ensign could quickly be given more responsibility for the actual running of the ship. It was seen as a means of quick advancement for those who had leadership skills and who did their jobs well.

Ross was assigned as damage-control officer, responsible for training the enlisted men in various safety drills, as well as preparing the ship and crew for any casualties and damage that might be sustained in combat. When the *Sigourney* left from Norfolk, Virginia, the Korean War was still in progress, though by the time the ship had reached Midway Island in the Pacific, a cease-fire had been declared and the war was over.

The ship continued on to the exotic ports of Hong Kong, Singapore, and Bangkok, Thailand. After months at sea, the young sailors on the destroyer were more than ready for shore leave (time off-duty in port). Perhaps because of his life-long abstention from alcohol, Ross was made the shore patrol officer, responsible for rounding up sailors who had gotten into fights, were drunk and disorderly, or otherwise were causing trouble. Of one colorful incident in a Mediterranean port, Ross recalls, "These guys were ready for liberty. I hauled more guys out of jail in the next two or three days than I ever will in my life. One guy got drunk, and decided to streak down the beach. I got a call to go and pick him up. It was a very funny sight, a young naval officer chasing a naked guy on the beach." Ross managed to wrap his coat around the sailor and haul him off to the brig.

Though Ross was thousands of miles away, the romance between he and Margot continued, mostly in the form of long letters the young navy man wrote describing exotic ports of call.

Margot graduated from Goucher College and began her own career as an elementary school teacher at nearby McDonogh School, and then as a third grade teacher at a boys' military school. Though she kept up correspondence with Ross, she was not yet certain she wanted to marry him. Her father, Donald Birmingham, had been much the same kind of man as Ross. A bank president with interests in politics and public policy, he was family-oriented, and had a strong, independent personality. Margot revered her father but wondered if Ross, her headstrong and determined suitor, would not be too much like her father.

Other similarities between the two families, however, pulled her toward Ross as a prospective bridegroom. Both the Perots and the Birminghams were close-knit clans with a strong sense of traditional values—hard work, fairness, and personal integrity. Like Lulu May Perot, Margot's mother Gertrude was a smart, capable woman who expected the best from her children. A Goucher graduate herself, she had majored in organic chemistry. Later, she was a teacher of Latin at the prestigious Mellon Institute in Pittsburgh, Pennsylvania.

The *Sigourney* kept going, visiting 22 countries during its nine-month cruise. While docked in Port Said, Egypt, Ross saw something that would haunt him for the rest of his life. In some parts of the Arab world, slavery was still legal. Close by the *Sigourney*, a ship bound for Arabia was busy loading its cargo—human beings, black slaves in chains being forced up a gangplank on their way to their new masters.

This sight shook Perot and many other sailors on board. "I just assumed we could do something," he said later, remembering the incident. In fact, he went to the captain and asked if the United States, the mightiest country in the world, could stop the sickening scene they were watching. But the captain could only shake his head.

By 1955, Ross had risen to the rank of chief engineer on the destroyer. But his career in the navy, which had begun so splendidly, was soon to take a downturn. A new captain took command of the *Sigourney*, and it was not long before a personality clash developed between the new boss and his young ensign.

Perot asked to be reassigned, and was transferred to the aircraft carrier *USS Leyte* as an officer in charge of gunnery control. Ross continued on the *Leyte*, and was later promoted to the position of assistant navigator.

Ross's sea duty was interrupted late in 1955 when his beloved father died after a long battle with heart disease. He flew home to Texarkana, where Margot Birmingham, realizing that Ross was now the most important man in her life, had joined the family for the funeral. Though his father's death was difficult for Ross, Margot's presence and support helped to alleviate his grief. As for her decision to accept Ross's continued request that they be married, she said "I knew that I could trust him. I knew that he was strong and honest. I knew that much. And I knew that life would never be dull if he was around. It may not sound romantic, but it was. He was an overwhelming presence."

Ross and Margot were married at her family home in September 1956. The honeymoon consisted of a motor trip; the newlyweds stayed at small inns along Skyline Drive, and splurged for one night at the Greenbriar Hotel, a resort in West Virginia where Margot's parents had honeymooned years before.

After the honeymoon, Ross reported to Quonset Naval Station, and the couple moved into a small furnished apartment in nearby Wickford, Rhode Island. The apartment only had three rooms, but the couple was happy in the small town atmosphere.

Margot got a job teaching in elementary school, and this helped to fill her time during the months when Ross shipped out. The newlyweds also watched their budget. "I put all my money in a savings account," recalls Margot. "Because we just didn't need it. We didn't spend much at all. The movies on the base were ten cents. And we'd go to the Officers' Club for dinner and not spend much. We'd buy what we needed and didn't worry."

Perot, however, had by that time become dissatisfied with the navy, and had changed his plan of a career as a military officer. Later in life, Perot would become one of the most staunch supporters of the military. But at this time he was troubled by the bureaucracy of the navy, by superior officers who were not always the best or brightest, and especially by how slowly careers advanced. His own advancement through the ranks would necessarily be slow and difficult, regardless of his initiative and hard work.

And here, as throughout his life, Ross was at the right place at the right time, and a seemingly chance event played an important part in his life. Because of his job as assistant navigator, Ross had become familiar with how computers operated. "I had touched a computer at a time when very few people had," he remembers. When a reserve officer who visited the *USS Leyte* happened to be an executive with International Business Machines (IBM), the computer giant, it was Ross's job to show the man around the ship. The executive was impressed by Perot, and urged the young ensign to apply for a job with IBM once his military duty was finished.

Though startled, Ross immediately replied, "Mister, you bet I'd like to have an interview with your company. I've worked since I was seven years old, and I'm 27 now, and you're the first person in my life to ever offer me a job." And so, the disgruntled young officer had accepted at least an informal offer for employment at IBM, one of the world's great corporations. Though, as he would admit later, at the time Ross had no idea what IBM did.

Although he thought about asking for an early release from the service, Perot continued his duties on the *Leyte*, was promoted to the rank of lieutenant, and finished his four-year tour of duty. He returned to civilian life with an honorable discharge in 1957. He was to serve an additional five years as a part-time officer in the Naval Reserve, but Ross knew that the tightly controlled life of a peace time navy was not for him. He needed a career that allowed him to use his intelligence, resourcefulness, and determination, one that rewarded him for the job he did, and not merely for the time he served. And Ross, as he left his ship for the last time, thought he had a job just like that waiting for him. He was going to work for IBM, one of the greatest success stories of American free enterprise.

COMPANY MAN

Fresh out of the Navy, Ross traveled to Hartford, Con-
necticut and took a variety of tests at IBM headquarters. The
executives were highly impressed with the young applicant,
who had the manner and bearing of a junior officer. Perot
was offered a job on the spot, to start work in Hartford. But
Ross, surprisingly, insisted he should be sent to the Dallas
office in his home state of Texas. It was a strange and
somewhat disconcerting request, but the IBM officials
finally agreed.

Though it would not be many years before Ross would
be a millionaire, the Perots lived a frugal life in Dallas.
Packing for the trip was not hard; almost everything fit into
the trunk of their 1952 Plymouth. Margot was a little
apprehensive about moving so far from home and the

environment she was accustomed to. "I was a little afraid of Texas. The size. That's what I first saw in 1957. It was during the big drought. It was absolutely flat and brown." However, she trusted Ross's judgment.

They rented a small duplex apartment for $125 a month. Ross made a deal with the landlord to lower the rent by ten dollars in exchange for cutting the grass and keeping the hedges trimmed. "We couldn't have been happier. Material things have nothing to do with happiness. We literally started with nothing," Ross remembers. The couple paid cash for everything they bought. Margot did their wash at a nearby Laundromat because a washer and dryer seemed a needless expense. Margot found work as a teacher, and they lived on Ross's salary and were able to bank her salary of $300 a month.

After a period of training, Ross got to work as the newest salesman in the Dallas office. With his close-cropped hair and neat military appearance, Ross fit right in with the other employees at IBM. Under the leadership of company founder Thomas Watson, IBM employees were all clean-shaven and wore dark suits with a white shirt and narrow tie, very much like a uniform. Watson believed that sales and customer service were the key to business success, and he had structured the company so that hard-working and innovative salespeople could make high commissions; but they were totally responsible for a customer's satisfaction. Ross believed in this dress-for-success and hard-work ethic, and would later use much the same approach as a model for his own business.

Though he was the new salesman in the office, Ross asked for the toughest assignments. He knew that the quickest way to learn the job, was to tackle the hardest tasks. His sales technique was simple. He would go away by himself, study everything he could find about the prospective customer, and then make his sales call. Although he never possessed an over-abundance of finesse as a salesman, Ross sold computers by convincing the customer that he understood his business, and had his best interest in mind.

In this era, computers were extremely large and expensive, although they were much less powerful than today's average desktop computer. The huge machines had little memory, and were programmed by inserting punch cards that contained the necessary instructions. Due to the primitive nature of the machines, each one had to be set-up for the specific business they were to be used in. An insurance company, for example, would need a much different system than a manufacturing plant.

The most successful IBM salesmen were those willing to spend long hours learning the intricacies of specific industries. Ross's willingness to work hard and to learn constantly was unequaled in the Dallas office. In one instance, Ross had a difficult time installing a system for a trucking firm, and actually moved a cot into the office so that he could work day and night until he mastered the job.

However, Ross eventually became unhappy at IBM. Much as he had when serving in the Navy, Ross bristled at the many layers of management. It simply did not suit his temperament to ask permission to try out every new idea that occurred to him. As he neared 30, he began to think about what his life would be like in the future if he continued to work for the computer giant. "If I'd stayed at IBM, I'd be somewhere in middle management getting in trouble and being asked to take early retirement," he said years later.

Ross's unhappiness with IBM increased when he was assigned a new boss, with whom he did not get along very well. He briefly considered transferring to the Los Angeles office, but decided he did not want to leave the state he loved.

Then Ross discovered the idea that would make him wealthy. He called the idea "facilities management," and it came to him because many of his potential customers resisted purchasing an expensive computer that would only be used for a limited number of hours each day. Always resourceful, Ross began putting two or three customers together to jointly buy a computer. It was a successful sales technique, and helped make Ross the highest producing salesman in IBM's Dallas office.

Then, other salesmen complained to management about Ross's strategy. They argued that Ross was actually hurting IBM, because it would be more profitable if every company purchased a computer, even if they could not use it efficiently. Ross, they complained, was hurting their sales by taking two or three customers out of the market while selling only one computer.

Ross had little patience with what he perceived as his fellow worker's jealousy, and he let his sales manager know how he felt. He thought it was silly for him to be reprimanded for finding a new way to sell computers. Besides, he argued, the companies he pooled together would not have purchased a computer on their own. That was why he pooled them in the first place.

To Ross's amazement, the manager supported the other salesmen, arguing that even if the companies would not have bought a computer now, they would have bought one in the future. Ross was too impatient, he said, and was giving up the potential for higher profits in the future for sales today.

Ross knew then, for certain, that he was not going to be happy at IBM, working in an environment where his initiative and problem solving skills were thwarted by jealousy and bureaucratic inertia. But, unwilling to give up on IBM yet, Ross kept his misgivings to himself.

Ross had learned something else from his customers. Many companies purchased a computer, often spending over a million dollars for the then state-of-the-art IBM 7070 mainframe, only to discover they had no practical idea of how to use it to help their business. In the early 1960s, few companies had employees skilled at installing the big machines, or in designing and writing the necessary software. The result was that many companies were more frustrated after buying a computer than they had been before.

Ross became convinced that a company specializing in setting up computer systems was needed. He envisioned a company of computer experts—installers, designers, programmers, and operators—who would contract with other companies to run their computer operations. Instead of making a profit from selling hardware, this new company would make money by selling skill and knowledge. What Ross called "facilities management," would later become known as data processing. Ross had anticipated the creation of a new industry.

IBM had the biggest pool of computer experts in the country. Ross's idea seemed like a natural new business for IBM. First sell the computer, then sell the people to run the computer. It was perfect, Ross thought. He presented his idea to his superiors.

But, management at IBM rejected his idea. The company was in the business of selling computers, they said, and was not concerned with what their customers did with the computers once they left the warehouse. And furthermore, his superiors reminded him, Ross was hired to sell equipment, not to create new divisions of IBM.

Ross grew more unhappy. Although he said later, "Things

were so good in those days at IBM that a salesman could get rich as long as he didn't get drunk during the day," Ross began to realize he wanted more out of life than a high salary and a cozy middle level management position at IBM. However, leaving a high paying job at IBM was not an easy decision. Margot had recently given birth to their first child, Ross Jr. He would be followed by four daughters: Nancy in 1960, Suzanne in 1964, Carolyn in 1968, and Katherine in 1971. And Ross was not wealthy. How could he start a computer services company when he did not even own a computer?

Two events finally motivated Ross to take the risk. The first was a new decision from IBM management in Dallas to limit the amount of commission one salesman could make in a year. Ross, by far the most successful salesman in the Dallas office, felt the commission cap was put into place to limit his income, because he was making more money than his boss. Ross was shocked that his ambition was being thwarted in this way.

The second event that pushed Ross out of IBM was more personal. He was sitting in the barber shop in Dallas, waiting to get a crew-cut, and reading an old *Reader's Digest.* "At the end of the stories they have these little one-liners," he remembers, "and they had Thoreau's quote, 'The mass of men lead lives of quiet desperation.' And I said, 'There I am.' " Ross realized, suddenly, that he had no alternative. If he did not start his own company, he would be miserable for his entire life.

Ross resigned from IBM on his thirty-second birthday, June 27, 1962, and took a thousand dollars from his and Margot's savings account to incorporate the new company he named Electronic Data Systems, or EDS. Finally, Ross was going to follow in his father's footsteps and own his own business.

EDS

Ross started Electronic Data Systems, the company that would make him one of the wealthiest men in America, with little money. He and Margot had only a modest bank account, accumulated by saving her teacher's salary. Ross originally had hoped to find investors who would take a chance on his idea for a new type of company. But, after being turned down repeatedly, Ross and Margot had to finance the new company themselves.

Ross was not overly discouraged when he failed to find investors. He knew he had a good idea, and he was willing to do what it took to make his idea a reality. He was confident the money would follow. "Brains and wits will beat capital all the time," Ross said later.

In the early years, EDS's headquarters was a single office Ross rented from a Dallas insurance company. He worked part-time for the insurance company, and spent the remainder of his day trying to find clients for his new company. Ross was hampered by one problem—he still did not own a computer. He had to convince clients that he and his employees could run their computer operations efficiently, and he also had to convince them to let EDS use the client's computer.

It was often a hard sale, but Ross showed the determination he later became famous for, and pursued clients relentlessly. At first only small customers signed up, and Ross sent in his new programmers and operators to solve the new client's computer problems.

Employees from the early days at EDS had to go the extra mile to make the company a success. Because they used the client's computer, most work had to be done at night. As the client's regular employees were leaving the office for the day, heading home to dinner with their families, EDS employees would be unloading boxes of computer tapes from the trunks of their cars, preparing for a night of programming and processing the company's data. As business grew, many EDS employees had to work on more than one project at a time, often spending the hours from 5:00 p.m. to 8:00 a.m. dashing from one worksite to another.

Ross is the first to admit that the success of EDS was due to the quality of the people he hired. In his view, success can be attributed to two things: "Good idea, great people." Potential employees were sought out one by one, and then put through an intensive interviewing process. Ross justified the effort he made searching out the right employees: "Eagles don't flock; you have to find them one at a time." Ross wanted people like him, self-starters, who were impatient with the slow-moving bureaucracies found in many corporations. Instead of hiring people who waited for the boss to tell them what to do, Ross wanted people who did what needed to be done on their own initiative. He offered smart, and mostly young, computer professionals a job that allowed them to work at their maximum potential.

Although EDS could not afford to pay the high salaries other computer companies, like IBM, could pay, and demanded long hours working in less than ideal conditions, the highly skilled work force grew rapidly. And once a new employee came to work, and made it through the intensive training program, he or she discovered that the motto around

Ross displays a piece of high-tech equipment used by EDS in 1968, a year before the company went public. (AP/Wide World Photos)

EDS was "Get it done." That was all Ross asked of them, but often it was tough to do.

Early EDS employees still remember Ross's gift for leadership. "He is one of the most unique people I have ever known, the type of fellow who could almost get you to jump off a cliff," one remembers. Another said years later: "If Ross asked me to drive to Alaska but he couldn't tell me why until I got there, I would be in my car an hour later."

But Ross also knew that people needed more than inspiration to motivate them. To compensate for the lower salaries EDS offered, Ross promised bonuses of company stock to employees. If a computer professional came to work for EDS, and performed well, he or she received stock as a bonus. Although at the time the stock was not worth much, Ross hoped his people would feel that their future wealth depended on the success of the company. Each employee was encouraged to think like an owner.

EDS quickly became known as a new type of company. Part of this reputation came from Ross's tendency to recruit young men who were leaving military service. Perhaps because of his own background, Ross liked to hire veterans. Veterans were often highly skilled, and many, like Ross, had received their education at one of the military academies.

Most had received the best computer training the U. S. Armed Forces could provide.

Also, veterans could more easily adjust to Ross's rules. Although Ross let his people perform their jobs with a minimum of hindrance from management, he did have some inflexible rules. Men could not have long hair, beards, or mustaches. The proper male dress was a dark suit with a crisp white shirt, a conservative tie, and dark, well-polished shoes. Women had to wear skirts or dresses. Jeans were outlawed. Ross said, "How much confidence would a bank or other client have in EDS if a representative of the company showed up in his office in jeans and a mop of uncut hair?" EDS employees were working with a company's most sensitive information. It was important that a bond of trust be established between the client and EDS. Ross thought conservative businessmen would more easily trust conservatively dressed computer professionals.

Over the years, Ross seemed amused, and sometimes irritated, by EDS's reputation as an ultra-conservative organization. "It's informal here," he said. "Anybody can come see me at any time. Everyone here can call me Ross. That is hardly a Nazi youth camp." But the image of EDS as a military-style company continued.

Other company rules reveal Ross's character, and the values his parents taught him. A married employee discovered having an affair was fired. Ross believed that an employee who would cheat on a spouse would also cheat on the job. Ross made each employee sign a pledge forbidding them to engage in any type of dishonest dealings, even if the dishonesty would favor EDS. Dishonesty simply was wrong, Ross said. EDS did not need profits that badly. There were more important things in life than money, and integrity was one of them.

EDS's first large account was the Frito Lay Company of Dallas. Frito Lay needed an accounting system for their route salesmen. Ross got the contract by proving he could save them half the money it would take to buy a computer from IBM and run it themselves. The Frito Lay project was a great success. Before long, EDS was doing business with the largest banks and insurance companies in Texas.

Three years after beginning his company, Ross was a millionaire. He had attained financial status beyond his biggest dreams. But EDS's phenomenal success was only beginning.

In 1965, Congress passed the Medicare program. Medicare was established to pay the health care costs of America's elderly citizens. Each hospital, doctor, and patient had to fill out forms to provide the government with information necessary to determine if the medical procedure met the Medicare guidelines. Insurance companies in each of the fifty states were awarded contracts from the federal government to process the Medicare forms.

Within months, the insurance companies were swamped in paper work, and the Medicare program was a mess. Hospitals and doctors either did not receive payment, or were paid twice for the same procedure. Elderly people were paying bills from their own pockets and then complaining to their representatives in Washington when they did not receive reimbursement. At some insurance companies, frustrated workers were simply boxing and storing unprocessed forms. The problem of Medicare reimbursement became so bad that many politicians started talking about eliminating the program.

Ross saw an opportunity. If a company could contract with the insurance companies to process the forms quickly and economically, there was almost no limit to the potential business. It was an opportunity to turn a crisis into EDS's big break.

The Texas Medicare system was as chaotic as any. Blue Cross and Blue Shield of Texas handled Medicare, and they were about to lose the state contract. Ross persuaded Blue Cross and Blue Shield's management to give EDS a chance to clear up the problems. When they agreed, Ross sent his best programmers and operators into the company's data processing center. After months of eighteen-hour work days, EDS had the state's Medicare program running smoothly.

Word of this success quickly spread throughout the Southwest, and eventually the entire country. EDS became known as the company that had solved Medicare data processing problems. The company grew at such a rapid rate that Ross's biggest problem was hiring enough people to do all the work. He and his team of recruiters began visiting colleges and military bases to search out the best prospects.

By 1968, EDS was processing the Medicare forms for 23 states. The company had over 350 employees, and business was still growing at a furious clip. Ross decided it was time to fulfill the promises he had made to the people who had come to work for him when he could not afford to offer them the salary they deserved. At the same time, he could turn himself into one of the wealthiest men in America.

Ross's decision was to "go public," to sell shares of company stock on the open market. The market would determine the value of EDS, and if the decision was positive, Ross and his employees would be very rich.

EDS went public in September of 1968, and Ross and the employees who had stuck with him over the years became wealthy. EDS stock initially sold for $16.50 a share, but within a year it was selling for $150.00 a share. Ross, who still owned 80% of EDS, had an estimated worth of $2 billion by the end of 1969. Many other employees were millionaires several times over.

Suddenly, the 38-year-old Ross was famous. Magazines began running stories of the short, young billionaire from Texas with the big ears. Interviewers began calling for quotes from him on all types of issues. Ross was usually happy to give them what they were looking for, and his brand of down-home humor made him even more widely known. When asked what he thought of young people with long hair, Ross, who still sported a crew-cut, quipped: "I have to be very careful there, because I have an extreme haircut, too. You know, it is a matter of personalities." On another occasion, he explained to *The Dallas Morning News* why he avoided doing business directly with the government, preferring to sub-contract from insurance companies instead: "Because, to the government, a horse is an animal with four legs, a head, and a tail, whether it's a jack-ass or a race horse." The legend of Ross Perot had begun.

Ross's fortune made him a favorite target of foundations and charities looking for contributions. Ross gave generously from the beginning, usually with the understanding that his gift would be anonymous. Occasionally, Ross allowed his name to be publicized, with the hope that others would be encouraged to do so by his example.

Although Ross was often a hard taskmaster, impatient and sometimes rude in the way he talked to people he did not feel were performing to their potential, he always supported his employees in a crisis. When one young man's newborn son was diagnosed with a severe heart condition, the doctors told the couple to expect the worse. Ross had the best heart surgeon in the country flown in to oversee the baby's care. The doctor found a way to save not only the baby's life, but to repair the problem. Ross paid all the bills.

In this case, he had never met the employee, who had only been with EDS a few months.

On another occasion, the wife of one of his programmers accidentally splashed drain cleaner into her eye. Ross saw to it that she received the best possible medical care, and her eye was saved. Sick children, traffic accidents, any family tragedy or crisis, could easily bring on an intense effort by Ross to help the stricken family through a difficult time. Ross gained a reputation as a tough but compassionate leader.

Ross also had a quirky side. One of his favorite tricks was to visit the homes of EDS employees during the day. He would drink coffee with the wife, tell her how much he appreciated the hard work her husband was doing for the company, and then would leave her with a gift of EDS stock. One housewife, whose husband had been working particularly long hours, received a stock gift that eventually became worth $400,000.

To many Americans, the enormous success of the little jug-eared man from Texas represented much of what they saw as great about America. But soon Ross would involve himself in a series of adventures, and misadventures, that earned him a reputation well beyond the business pages. Ross threw himself into the middle of an issue that was threatening to divide the people of the United States—the war in Vietnam.

MISSION TO HANOI

As the 1960s drew to a close, the war in Vietnam developed into a divisive issue. The United States had become involved in the conflict when the communist government of North Vietnam attempted to overthrow the pro-American government of South Vietnam. At first, the fighting was generally supported by the American people. But, as the war intensified, and the United States government sent increasingly larger numbers of soldiers to fight, the war became more controversial. By 1969, many Americans thought the United States should get out of Vietnam, and they marched and protested to let the nation's leaders know how they felt.

Some anti-war activists lost patience with Americans who agreed to fight in Vietnam, and accused them of killing innocent Vietnamese. For the first time in American history, returning war veterans were not cheered by their fellow citizens.

If the treatment the Vietnam veterans received by some of their fellow citizens was sometimes unfair, many thought the United States government was treating them even worse. As it became clear the war was not going to be won militarily, some political leaders wanted only to distance themselves from America's first defeat. Many soldiers in Vietnam, and their supporters at home, grew bitter at the lack of support they received from their government. Nothing pointed out this bitterness more than the issue of the American prisoners of war, or POWs, held in North Vietnam.

Ross was one of the Americans deeply concerned about the POWs. Although Ross had decided a military career was not for him, he remained devoted to the men and women who served in the military. In 1969, he had an opportunity to show how concerned he really was.

By the end of the 1960s, Ross was well known in Washington. He contributed large amounts of money to Richard Nixon's campaign for President in 1968. When

Nixon won by a slim majority of votes, many in the new administration, including President Nixon, were grateful to Ross for his help. Ross had a reputation in the Nixon White House as a man who could be trusted to do what he promised to do.

Henry Kissinger, Nixon's National Security Advisor, called Ross from the White House in 1969 and asked him to come to a meeting in Washington D.C. Ross agreed.

Washington in 1969 was a city in turmoil. Almost weekly, anti-war protesters held rallies in front of the White House, or in nearby Lafayette Park. The crowds at the anti-war protests were not only made up of young people. Increasingly, older Americans decided they did not want their sons or daughters to serve in a war no one expected to win. President Nixon knew every statement he made about Vietnam would be controversial. He was hemmed in politically. The POWs, held in near-inhuman conditions in North Vietnamese prison camps, was one issue the President wanted to settle.

Henry Kissinger explained the President's problem to Ross during their meeting in Washington, and told him the President needed his help. As Ross reported later, Kissinger

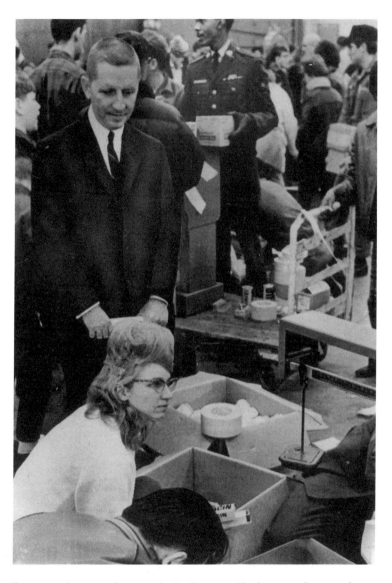

Perot watches as volunteers in Anchorage, Alaska, repackage a plane load of Christmas parcels he was attempting to deliver to American POWs in North Vietnam. (AP Wide/World Photos)

told him: "Our intelligence reports say that half the POWs in Vietnam will die of brutality or neglect before the war is over. Can you help us?" After checking to make sure his efforts would not break any laws, Ross agreed to do what he could.

Perot decided the best strategy would be to embarrass the North Vietnamese in the eyes of the world. Most nations had decided, and some had stated publicly, that it was wrong for the United States to be fighting in Vietnam. Perhaps revealing to the world how the North Vietnamese were treating American soldiers would win support from other countries, and from the anti-war protesters at home.

Ross planned a series of public events to focus attention on the POW issue. For the first event he decided to charter two planes, fill them with Christmas presents and mail from loved ones, and attempt to deliver the cargo to POWs held in camps in Hanoi, the capital of North Vietnam.

There were problems from the beginning. Ross needed two large jets with enough cargo room to transport all the presents. But it was the Christmas season, and all available charter planes were already reserved. To the amazement of others working on the project, Ross offered to buy two planes. He had difficulty convincing them he was not joking. But before Ross had to buy two jets, two Boeing 707s were located and leased.

Ross loaded the two planes with letters, gifts, food, and medicine. The mission was ready to go; the planes took off. Then the North Vietnamese created a different problem. Although they had previously agreed to let the planes land, they added a new condition at the last minute. Supposedly for security reasons, no large packages could be delivered. The largest package they would accept was nine inches by twelve inches.

Word of the new requirement reached Ross when the planes landed in Anchorage, Alaska, for refueling. At first it looked like a fatal blow. There was not enough time to repackage two jet cargo bays full of presents and make the Christmas Day deadline earlier established by the North Vietnamese. Then something Ross later came to see as a near-miracle happened. As word spread throughout the city of the problem, the airport hangar filled with local volunteers who worked all night re-packaging the presents. The planes left next morning on schedule.

Then the North Vietnamese radioed the approaching planes that they could not land in Hanoi. The delivery of presents and medicine would have to be delivered to Moscow, in what was then the Soviet Union. The Soviets would be in charge of delivering the presents to the POWs, Hanoi said. Although it meant the families on the planes would not be allowed to see their loved ones, Ross had no choice but to deliver the presents to Moscow.

Ross's next attempt to attract attention to the plight of the POWs got him in trouble with the Nixon Administration. When they had asked Ross for his help, Kissinger and Nixon expected Ross to be under their control. They believed in pursuing a quiet style of diplomacy. They thought it was best not to create a public controversy over an issue, and preferred to work behind the scenes. Much to the Nixon's Administration's dismay, they discovered Ross did not agree with their "go slowly and quietly" strategy.

Ross believed quiet diplomacy had been given its chance and had failed. "They [the United States government] told the wives and mothers, 'The less said the better; just don't ripple the waters,'" Ross said later. "They'd been saying that for so long, we decided that the best way to handle it was just the opposite. Say something. Ripple the waters."

Ross paid to have 150 POW relatives flown to Paris, where the United States and the North Vietnamese were holding negotiations to end the war. The relatives did not attempt to interrupt the negotiations, but they hung around in the background and the hallways while the diplomats met, and held press conferences to tell the world how the North Vietnamese were mistreating the POWs.

Ross had other ideas on how to free the POWs. A few months after the Christmas flights, Ross invited families of the prisoners as well as journalists to accompany him on another flight to Hanoi. The North Vietnamese officials refused to meet with him. There was also a story in the United States media of Ross making a personal $100 million offer to the North Vietnamese in return for release of the prisoners.

The $100 million story may have been no more than a rumor. By this time, early in 1970, Ross's image in the media had began to change. Earlier, he had been portrayed as an entrepreneurial genius. But Vietnam was a complicated and divisive issue, and most people's attitude toward Ross's public efforts in support of the POWs were determined by their opinion of the Vietnam War. If someone supported America's involvement in the war, they usually supported Ross's efforts. Those not supporting the war usually saw Ross as an ultraconservative kook.

Ross talking with North Vietnam POWs at Bien Hoa, South Vietnam, in 1970. (AP/Wide World Photos)

Ross and wife Margot check the rising price of EDS stock on a ticker tape machine in 1971. (AP/Wide World Photos)

Ross weathered the criticism with his usual resilience. But to the Nixon Administration, Ross had become a problem. They had not counted on his public campaign to gain world attention. He was much too flamboyant; he made the State Department diplomats nervous. Many in the White House, including Henry Kissinger, began to distance themselves from Ross's efforts. A State Department spokesman called Ross "eccentric," strong words for a diplomat.

Ross had had his first taste of how Washington worked. It would not be his last.

Although Ross's efforts to help the POWs were not a total success, they were not a complete failure either. The publicity he generated focused many Americans' attention on the issue. More people realized the immense difficulties that were involved in extricating the United States from the war. As the release of the POWs became more critical to the peace agreement being negotiated in Paris, the U. S. negotiators discovered that Ross's efforts helped them persuade Americans to be patient. Most were willing to wait for an agreement that guaranteed the safe return of the prisoners. Ross's work helped give the negotiators time to get the best agreement possible.

Perhaps the best thing Ross gained personally from the experience was the opportunity to meet Army Green Beret Colonel Arthur D. "Bull" Simons. Simons, who had a tougher-than-nails personality, was a legendary solider. When, in November of 1970, Simons led a group of commandos that attacked the Son Tay prison camp outside of Hanoi, in a brave but unsuccessful effort to free American POWs, he became a national symbol of the best type of American solider. Simons became a hero to those working to free the American prisoners. After the raid, Ross asked to meet the Son Tay Raiders, and was invited to Fort Bragg, North Carolina, where he met Colonel Simons. After the war, Perot threw a gigantic party for the Son Tay Raiders in San Francisco to show his appreciation for their efforts. Ross invited the actor John Wayne, who had starred in the movie *The Green Berets*, to the party. When Wayne met Simons he said, "You're the man I play in the movies."

Simons was deeply grateful to Ross. They formed a friendship that Perot would call on a few years later, in another dramatic crisis.

IRANIAN RESCUE

Although busy with public affairs, Ross guided EDS into the 1970s. As the company became the largest data processing company in the United States, Ross knew that future growth might depend on how much business the company could contract from overseas. Many countires lagged behind the U.S. in computer services. They needed help entering the computer age. Ross pushed EDS into becoming an international corporation.

One of the countries EDS began doing business with was Iran. In the 1970s, Iran was ruled by the Shah Pahlevi. The Shah had come to power in a coup in 1953, and had struggled during his reign to win the support of his people.

The Shah's strategy to maintain his power had two elements. He used the money from Iran's oil sales to buy weapons and to hire military advisors from the United States and other countries. Iran built the largest and best equipped army in the Middle East. He also trained a secret police organization, called the SAVAK, to frighten people into submission.

To placate the frightened subjects, the Shah also spent vast sums of money to create public programs. One was a social security system, modeled after the American system. Social Security provides a pension for retired and disabled citizens.

As the Iranian social security system grew, it became clear the old methods of record keeping were inadequate. The Iranian Ministry of Health, which ran the system, needed help with data processing. To Ross and others at EDS, the Iranian problems were similar to the Medicare problems they had successfully solved. EDS decided to bid for the Iranian contract.

Ross and the other EDS managers worked hard to acquire the contract. Ross called people he knew in Washington. He did not hesitate to ask for help from his well-connected friends. But he refused to pay bribes to Iranian bureaucrats in order to secure the contract. Although this was an accepted business custom in many parts of the world, Ross went so far as to require all his employees to sign an agreement promising never to pay bribes in return for business.

As it turned out, bribes were not needed. EDS was the best data processing company in the world. It won the contract to set-up the computer system inside the Iranian Ministry of Health. But, before much time had passed, Ross would regret winning the Iranian contract.

Landing in Teheran, the Iranian capital, in the summer of 1976, the EDS employees started their work as they did all new jobs. Computerizing an entire nation's records was a massive undertaking and, enthusiastic to prove themselves, they worked long hours.

There were problems from the beginning. The initial troubles resulted from the clash of two different cultures. The EDS spirit was that hard work could solve any problem. However, the Iranian employees of EDS, and the Ministry of Health officials, worked differently. When a problem developed, the American employees wanted to jump on it and come up with a solution. The Iranians usually wanted to put the problem off to another time, or break for tea, or have a meeting in the future. This clash of working styles discouraged many on the EDS team.

Other problems were even more out of EDS's control. By 1977, the dramatic increases in the price of oil that had begun with the 1973-74 oil embargo, had slowed. The Shah and his advisors suddenly realized they did not have the money to pay for many of the social and military changes they had already put into place. The Shah turned to western banks for loans, but this increased inflation, which made the financial situation worse. Iran had not planned for the day when the easy oil money dried up.

EDS began having trouble receiving payment for its work. Ministry of Health officials stopped returning phone calls. Efforts in Teheran, and from the Dallas headquarters, to collect the money brought on veiled threats by Ministry officials. When EDS informed the Ministry of Health they would stop work, shutting down the social security system, they were told that such an act would result in severe punishment, perhaps even imprisonment of the Americans working in the country. In other words, they could not stop working, but they would not be paid for the work they did. This was not the way EDS customarily did business.

The situation grew worse. As the economy deteriorated,

protests against the hated government grew more violent. The Shah's extravagant lifestyle made the people even more angry during the bad times.

The Shah's most powerful enemy was the Muslim clergy, especially the exiled Ayatollah Khomeini. Iranians were predominantly Shiite Muslims, and there is a centuries-old tradition among Shiites of opposing governments they felt were not based on the *Koran*, the holy book of Islam. The Shah, with his close ties to the United States, and his western lifestyle, which the Iranian clergy saw as decadent, was hated by many of Iran's religious leaders. Over the years, the Shah had made the situation even worse by arresting, imprisoning, and sometimes executing his enemies among the clergy.

The Ayatollah Khomeini was the most revered of the Shiite clergymen. Forbidden for years by the Shah from visiting Teheran, living in exile in the city of Oman, Iran, Khomeini had developed a deep hatred of the Shah. Khomeini was a gifted writer and speaker who was able to use his knowledge of the *Koran* to win thousands of Iranians to his side. When Khomeini's son was killed by SAVAK in the early 1970s, most observers knew that either Khomeini or the Shah would not survive the struggle.

Many of the Shah's supporters were lulled into a false sense of security when Khomeini left Iran and moved to Paris. But Khomeini had left hundreds of trained lieutenants in Iran, many of whom would consider it a great honor to die for the cause. In addition, Khomeini began making cassette tapes of his sermons and speeches. These tapes were duplicated and smuggled back into Iran by the thousands, where they became popular among the youth. When the Shah's economic troubles began hurting the people of Iran, Khomeini's voice was there to encourage them toward revolution.

While the revolution was developing, EDS continued negotiating a financial settlement with the Ministry of Health. In the middle of discussions, the Ministry claimed that EDS owed them money.

Negotiations dragged on. Non-essential EDS employees quietly began leaving Iran, as threats of lawsuits and counter-lawsuits continued between Dallas and Teheran. Ross knew the Ministry officials were in a bad position. They did not have the money to pay EDS, but they could not allow the social security system to collapse, which would drive additional thousands of angry people onto the volatile streets. A total collapse of the Shah's government would put the Ministry officials' own lives at risk, because Khomeini's hatred for the Shah extended to the people who worked in the government.

Finally, Ministry of Health officials arrested two of EDS's top managers. The men, Paul Chiapparone and Bill Gaylord, were charged with corruption, and thrown into a prison in central Teheran. Bail was set at 13 million dollars, the amount the Ministry insisted EDS owed them. In effect, Ross's employees were being held hostage.

When Ross received word on December 28, 1978, that the two men were being held hostage, he immediatley started working to get them out. But, he had no idea how difficult that was going to be. The first thing Ross did was to contact the U.S. State Department, expecting them to free the men by diplomatic means. The charges against Chipparone and Gaylord were obviously trumped up. Ross's reputation as an honest businessman had never been questioned, and he had made certain everyone knew that EDS did not pay bribes, or engage in any type of corruption.

At first, the State Department refused to talk to Ross. Then, they told EDS lawyers that they had no power to intervene in an Iranian criminal investigation. All they could do was to contact the Iranian Embassy in Washington and ask that the men not be harmed. When Ross protested that the men had done nothing to justify imprisonment, the State Department's response was that an Iranian court would have to make that judgment.

Ross was angry. His employees were being held hostage, and their own government would not even attempt to free them. But, when his anger cooled, he decided to pay the ransom. It went against his nature, but the safety of his employees, both of whom had families with small children, was more important. He began negotiating a way to pay the money. Using cash to pay the ransom was out of the question. Flying into turbulent Iran with 13 million dollars in cash would put the courier's life in danger; and what was to stop the Iranians from simply taking the money, and then continuing to refuse to release the men?

The ransom would have to be paid by some sort of check, or letter of credit. But no bank would guarantee a letter of credit to an Iranian bank, because of the possibility the bank would be seized by the followers of Khomeini, who would then refuse to honor the debt. It began to seem to Ross that the more he negotiated, the more problems he encountered. Finally, the Iranians at the Ministry of Health told EDS lawyers that even if the "bail" was paid the men would not be allowed to leave until after they were tried. Paying the ransom would not result in the men coming home.

Ross's efforts to free the men through normal procedures had failed for a basic reason: the Iranian government no longer had any power. He had been wasting his time talking with people who could not deliver on their promises. There were only two alternatives left. Ross could walk away from the men, and leave them to take their chances in Teheran. Or he could find a way to break them out of prison.

Most of Ross's top advisors tried to talk him out of attempting to rescue the men. They pointed out first, that such an attempt was illegal. Second, Ross would have to risk several other lives to attempt to save two men. Then, failure of the mission could even destroy his business. But Ross was undeterred. He understood the risk. But the men worked for him, and he felt responsible for their being in Iran. He was willing to take the responsibility to get them out.

For Ross, there was only one man to take charge of a rescue mission — Colonel "Bull" Simons, who had retired from the army. Deeply unhappy since the death of his wife, he jumped at the chance to help fellow Americans. His only question was: "When do we start?"

Simons came to Dallas and began training a select group of eight EDS employees, most of whom were veterans of the Vietnam War. The group drilled in the fundamentals of combat, and planned the raid they codenamed Operation HOTFOOT, an acronym for Help Our Two Friends Out Of Teheran.

Operation HOTFOOT's original plan concentrated on freeing the men from prison. The prison was not heavily guarded, and was surrounded only by a low wall. Each rescuer had specific assignments, but the plan essentially involved scaling the walls, seizing the guards, whisking the two men out of their cells, and fleeing toward the Turkish border.

The rescue team broke into small groups. Some entered Teheran, others went to Turkey to arrange help for the border crossing. The rescuers in Teheran were disturbed by what they saw around them. Gunfire echoed in the streets at all hours; social order had collapsed. Then, shortly after their arrival, the Shah announced he was leaving Iran for a vacation; no one expected him to return. With the collapse of the government, the rescue team knew their fellow employee's lives were in serious danger. They tried to keep their spirits up, and began purchasing vehicles and other equipment necessary for their mission.

Ross boosted the men's spirits when he masqueraded as a video tape courier for NBC News and sneaked into Teheran. He even visited the two imprisoned men, and promised them they would be freed. Ross stayed in Teheran several days, until he was convinced that his presence put the entire mission at risk.

Shortly after Ross left the city, the hostages were moved from the minimum security facility to the maximum security Qasr Prison. All plans of scaling walls and seizing guards were now useless. The EDS men on the rescue squad were dejected.

But not Bull Simons. The old warrior boosted their morale by saying it was inevitable that the people of Teheran would eventually attack the prison to free the Iranian inmates, most of whom were being held on political charges. Storming the Bastille Prison had been the climactic moment of the French Revolution, he said. The same thing would happen here. All they had to do was wait for the mob to act. Then, they could collect the hostages and flee the country.

On Sunday, February 11, 1979, a mob in Teheran, whipped into a frenzy by the recent return of the Ayatollah Khomeini, stormed Qasr Prison. The two EDS employees walked out of the prison in the confusion and bribed taxi drivers to take them across the chaotic city, where they joined the rescue team at the Hilton Hotel.

Although the men were out of prison, it was too soon to begin celebrating. To Iran, the two men were still worth 13 million dollars; dozens of soldiers and police would soon be roaming the streets looking for them. Escaping the prison had been the easy part.

Half the rescue team left by plane. The other half, including the two hostages and an Iranian guide, bought two Land Rover vehicles and headed for the Turkish border, five hundred miles away.

The revolution had spread out from Teheran, and the entire countryside was in turmoil. Sections of Iran were still controlled by pro-Shah forces; if the team were caught, they all would be arrested and possibly killed. Other parts of Iran were controlled by the rebels, mostly young men and boys

Perot, freed hostages Bill Gaylord and Paul Chiapperone, and retired Colonel Arthur "Bull" Simons in Dallas after the successful escape from Iran in 1979. (AP/Wide World Photos)

loyal to Khomeini. These young radicals viewed all Americans as the enemy, and would not hesitate to shoot them.

The trip across western Iran was slow and perilous. The group was stopped repeatedly, and often interrogated by soldiers on both sides of the conflict. Once they even had to convince pro-Khomeini troops they were all working for Khomeini. Finally, they reached the Turkish-Iranian border. They could see the bus Ross had hired on the Turkish side of the guarded fence. Freedom was in sight. Then the border guards refused to allow them to drive across the border. Thinking quickly, the men climbed out of the expensive Land Rovers, and headed toward the border on foot. When the guards realized the vehicles were being left for them to keep, they let the men escape. On February 15, 1979, the men were free.

When the group finally reached the U.S., and the story of their rescue became known, Ross became famous. During the next several months, the situation in Iran continued to deteriorate; Americans working in the U. S. Embassy in Teheran were taken hostage and subsequently held for 440 days. The rescue of the EDS hostages became a symbol to many Americans of the type of action American government could and should take.

Ross tried to make sure the rescue team, especially Bull Simons, got most of the credit for the rescue. Simons, in his gruff way, appreciated the adulation he received. But his days of glory were short-lived. Bull Simons died on May 21, 1979, three months after returning from Iran. He lived out his last weeks in a guest cottage on Ross's estate. When he died, Ross arranged for a hero's funeral.

LONE STAR CRUSADER

After the successful freeing of the EDS hostages, and the publicizing of the rescue mission in the best-selling book, *On Wings Of Eagles*, by British thriller writer Ken Follett, Ross became a national hero. In a country reeling from the setbacks of the Vietnam War and the Watergate scandal, Ross was a symbol of old-fashioned American ingenuity, a man who took direct action for a worthy cause.

Ross was most famous in his native Texas, where EDS was a major employer. With his ready quips and no-nonsense manner, he became an even more influential man in Texas public affairs.

During the 1980s, public education reform became a hotly debated issue in Texas. Although Texas was a wealthy state, public school students consistently scored near the bottom on standardized tests. While it was an embarrassment to the citizens of Texas, inadequate education also threatened the economic future of the state.

Ross, who had made his fortune in a high-technology business, knew young people had to be prepared for the future high-tech economy. When Governor Mark White asked Ross to head a committee to analyze public education in Texas, Ross devoted several months to the effort.

Ross's committee proposed drastic reforms, including higher teacher salaries, three years of pre-school for poor children, the testing of teachers, and salary raises on a strict merit plan. The most controversial reform was a no-pass, no- play rule for student athletes, which meant the athletes had to maintain passing grades in order to participate in school sporting activities.

Many state legislators, and the education establishment, were shocked by these proposals. They had not expected such a radical reform package. Most had expected Ross to propose moderate changes that would not cost much money. Instead, Ross had proposed a massive series of reforms that would cost $8 billion. Perot again became a center of controversy.

Ross did not shrink from the fight. In his interviews and speeches he continued to shock Texans. When speaking about the need to raise teacher's pay in order to recruit more qualified college students into the teaching profession, Ross said: "The dumbest folks in college are studying to be teachers." In defending his get-tough attitude on high school sports, Ross joked: "I thought I was living pretty well until I found out that high school football players have towel warmers."

Ross also attacked vocational education, such as agriculture studies, as a way for students to avoid tougher, academic classes. To prove his point that too often agriculture classes were actually "crip" courses for lazy students, Ross used the story of the boy and the chicken to make his point. "I have a documented case of one boy who traveled 35 days across Texas with a chicken. Everyone wants to know why the boy came home? The chicken was worn out. A chicken can only take so much travel."

Ross's educational reform campaign also used citizen lobbyists. Supporters of the plan, some of them paid, others volunteers, followed state legislators around, seizing on every opportunity to push for the committee's reforms.

"Letters to the Editor" sections of the state's newspapers were filled with encouragement and support for the new programs.

However, the reforms had strong opposition. Teachers threatened to boycott the competency tests. Football coaches spoke out against the no-pass no-play rule. Those who wanted lower taxes also spoke out against the cost of improving education standards.

Ross and his supporters fought on, and the education package was passed in the summer of 1984. Ross had his political victory. However, the fight for education reform taught Ross another bitter lesson about politics. Even after a bill passes a legislature, there is no guarantee that the expected results will take place.

Because of teacher protests, and the fear that many football coaches would not pass it, the teacher's competency test was made so simple that only one percent of the teachers failed. Wealthier school districts protested the state's plan to shift money to the poorer districts, and took their case to court. And most importantly, the legislature refused to fully fund the reforms. Today, Texas still ranks near the bottom among states in education, with low Scholastic Aptitude Test scores and high dropout rates.

Ross had run head-on into a problem that was, in many ways, resistant to the leadership style he used at EDS. Education reform does not happen quickly, and charismatic leadership only goes so far in government. Ross was discovering that public policy issues were, in many ways, more difficult than building a multi-billion dollar corporation, or rescuing hostages from a foreign country.

Fighting drug abuse also occupied Ross's time in the 1980s. For years, drug abuse has been a major problem in American society, especially among young people. When Texas politicians asked Ross to help solve the problem, Ross asked lawyers who worked for EDS to help him draft laws for the legislature to consider.

Ross proposed getting tougher on drug pushers: "You can declare civil war and the drug dealer is the enemy. There ain't no bail. . . You can start to deal with the problem in straight military terms. We can apply the rules of war." He advocated mandatory sentences for anyone convicted of selling drugs. People convicted of selling drugs to children would get a mandatory life term in prison.

Ross also asked for public education of parents about the dangers of drug abuse. His drug task force established an office in Austin, the Texas capital, to implement the drug education policy. The program was successful, and then-first lady Nancy Reagan used it as a model for her famous "Just Say No" campaign.

As usual, many of Ross's suggestions were controversial. He thought pharmacists should be required to report on all prescriptions filled for restricted drugs; paint and glue sales should be curtailed to keep youngsters from becoming addicted to inhaled fumes; police should be given a wider authority to wiretap suspected drug offenders. Perhaps most controversial of all, he advocated that people who lived in areas where drug abuse was endemic should have their houses and persons searched without requiring the police to attain a warrant. Ross suggested the "drug war" was a real war, and that some constitutional protections should be put aside in order to gain total victory.

The Texas legislature passed some of these proposals. However, druggists and drug companies were able to stop the restrictions on pharmaceutical sales, and limited prison space made it necessary to water down some of the mandatory sentencing requirements. But drug laws were tightened, especially the laws regarding the selling of drugs to children. Ross did not win on all counts, but he did succeed on focusing attention on the problem of drug abuse, and many of the suggestions he made had an impact on the developing national policy toward illegal drugs.

Ross was able to fit a good amount of fatherhood into his increasingly busy and high-powered business life. Ross Jr. recalls that his dad would take him along on business errands, just as G. R. Perot had taken young Ross into the business world outside the home many years before. "He always included me any time he could. . . which is very important, for a young boy to watch his father."

Ross Jr. would grow to adulthood much taller and heavier than his dad, and with some of the more refined personality traits of his mother, but the emphasis on family discipline did not change from the Texarkana home of Ross Sr.'s youth. As were the rest of the children, Ross Jr. was taught discipline and respect for his elders, to say "yes sir" and "no ma'am," just as his father was taught. Ross Jr. recalls: "Dad was the head of the house. He had strong principles and set out the rules. Mom had the same principles and made sure we toed the line."

Although he was one of the country's most well-known businessmen, Perot had prided himself on being a family man. He has always found time for his children. "He was a very loving dad," recalls Margot. "When the kids were little they would go riding with him, sit in front of him on the saddle, and make up stories."

Two incidents show how concerned and caring Ross was about his children. As a fourth grader, Carolyn was stumped by a science project for a school fair which was due the next day. Ross stayed up until dawn, helping his daughter until the project was completed. Carolyn, with her father's help, won a second prize for the assignment.

At another time, the collie dog that was a favorite of Suzanne's ran off the property. When it failed to come home, she was distraught. Ross borrowed one of the children's bicycles and rode through the surrounding neighborhoods, with no luck. Finally, he hand-painted an armful of "lost dog" signs, offered a reward, and plastered them at nearby stores and shopping centers. His concern paid off, and the dog was located and returned to the home.

Perot was careful to keep his private life separate from his public life, and his home as a safe and special place for all the family. Ross Jr. recalls: "He never talked about what he did. At dinner he would make one of us talk about our activities. The world revolved around us."

Perot's family was growing up. And though Margot and Ross demanded the best education for their children (Ross Jr. attended exclusive St. Mark's, a private school for boys, and the girls all went to the Hockaday School, an elite girl's academy), they were not pampered or coddled, as one might expect the children of a billionaire to be. Ross Jr. received allowances of only a quarter or fifty cents a week, though the family lived on a sprawling estate. Daughter Nancy recalls, "We were encouraged to achieve through work, and there was never any emphasis on material goods or wealth."

DISSENTER IN DETROIT

In April of 1984, while busy with Texas education reform, Ross received a phone call that would change his life.

The call was from the chairman of Salomon Brothers, one of the largest investment banks in New York City. Investment banks make money by brokering the buying and selling of companies. Ross could not understand why Salomon Brothers wanted to talk to him. EDS was not for sale. But when the chairman, John Gutfreund, asked to come to Dallas to visit Ross, Ross agreed.

When Gutfreund arrived the next day, he made a proposal that forced Ross to re-consider his decision not to sell his company. General Motors, the largest corporation in the world, wanted to buy EDS. After consulting with his advisors, Ross decided to consider the offer.

There was one question Ross wanted answered. GM seldom bought other companies, preferring to create new divisions within their company. The policy of growing internally had allowed the company to keep its corporate debt low. Although they had lost a share of the automobile market to imports from Japan and Europe during the 1980s, low debt had kept the auto maker profitable. Now GM was approaching Ross with an offer to buy, breaking a long-standing policy. Ross wondered why.

The answer to Ross's question was in the mind of Roger Smith, Chairman of General Motors. Smith had assumed control of the automaker at a tough time in its history. Profits were falling, as was corporate prestige, when cars like the Chevrolet Vega and Cavalier suffered low sales. Smith decided GM had grown complacent, and needed to be shaken out of its doldrums with the injection of a hard-driving, can-do attitude. Smith thought Ross Perot and his company would provide that attitude.

Smith told Ross his ideas during their first meeting. After Smith made his bid, Ross told him he thought it was a mistake for him to buy EDS. "I told Roger at the end of the first day, 'Roger, you don't have to buy a dairy to get the milk. . . We'll sell you service,' " Ross said later.

Smith, however, remained determined to buy EDS. Ross could not easily reject the offer. As a boy in Texarkana, the Chevrolet, Buick, and Cadillac dealerships were where prosperous people bought their new cars. During his youth, owning a Cadillac, the top GM luxury car, was the ultimate symbol of accomplishment. To Ross, an offer from General Motors was different than an offer from any other company.

Ross was also deeply worried about the condition of America's manufacturing industries, especially the once world-dominant automobile business. He agreed with Smith that American business needed to be shaken up. They both felt that the growth of middle-level management resisted change. Both thought this "frozen middle," as Smith called it, was even a greater threat than were imports.

But Perot was not star-struck by the offer. Several times it looked as though the deal would fall apart. Ross was a tough negotiator, and insisted on maintaining control of all computer operations; GM would create a separate stock to represent the value of EDS; and profits would be calculated internally, so that if the larger company lost money and EDS made money, Ross's wealth would not suffer. Smith reluctantly agreed to each demand.

Ross also made other demands that later became the source of tension with Roger Smith. Ross wanted a seat on the Board of Directors; his management team could not be changed; and pay and bonuses for Ross's employees should be decided by him. And finally, EDS could earn a 9% profit for all work it did for GM. Ironically, Smith agreed to these demands immediately.

The deal was made. Perot sold the company he started on his birthday, June 27, 1984, exactly twenty-two years from the day of its founding. If Ross was sad about selling the company he had built into a giant corporation, he did not express his feelings publicly. He talked to reporters of his excitement at having the chance to help the flagship company of American industrial might.

Ross blew into Detroit, the center of the American automobile industry, like a Texas tornado—and ran into a brick wall.

The trouble began when the EDS representatives made their first contact with the GM workers now under their control. The men and women in GM's data processing departments were used to their way of doing things, which did not include long hours, quick decisions, and rapid changes. In addition, most of the middle managers had earned promotions by aligning themselves with superiors, and now those relationships were broken.

The former GM employees refused to change. Ken Reidlinger, the man Ross assigned to oversee the merger, held meeting after meeting to lay out plans and proposed new ideas for working more efficiently. The data processing managers sat quietly through the meetings, then went back to their offices and continued on as though the meeting had never taken place.

Perot and Reidlinger decided to hire new workers. They hoped the new employees would shake up the old GM people. But the tactic only angered them more. The new workers also brought Ross into his first conflict with Roger Smith. Smith complained about the additional salaries. Ross responded that more people were needed to handle all the new work.

Then GM's finance department complained that EDS should get their approval for any new investments in computers. Ross explained to Smith that the new equipment was necessary to handle the increased work. After a struggle, Smith gave in. Ross, however, began to have doubts about Smith's devotion to shaking up the giant company.

The internal problems grew. GM managers began telling reporters it was more like EDS had bought General Motors, instead of the other way around. The fundamental problem was a clash of two very different companies. GM was an old fashioned, top-down organization. A career could be ruined by making one wrong decision, so most ambitious executives tried to avoid making any decisions at all, especially ones advocating change. At EDS, making no decision was worse than making the wrong decision. Smith had thought buying the new company could change decades of tradition.

An even larger problem developed in the corporate relationship. Ross attracted reporters wherever he went, and he did not hesitate to use the media to push his ideas. Ross wanted to transform the giant automaker. Ross told reporters he had no intention of playing corporate politics, that he intended to be an advocate for the dealers, workers and shareholders. He hung a painting of a marine in his office

Ross with his beloved wife, Margot, in 1987.

to remind GM management he thought the job was to beat back the flood of Japanese imports that were hurting sales. Many on the Board of Directors were offended by Ross's comments.

In April of 1985, Ross visited a Cadillac dealer's convention. The dealers told him that management did not discuss future plans with them. Ross publicly said he thought this policy was foolish and inexcusable. When Smith heard of Ross's comments, he let his displeasure be known. Ross was unruffled by Smith's anger. Smith discovered Ross did not "play pussyfoot." If he disagreed, he let everyone know it. Relations between Ross and Smith grew strained.

The issue that split Perot and Smith's relationship beyond repair was Smith's decision to buy Hughes Aircraft. Hughes was a defense contractor, originally founded by legendary business tycoon Howard Hughes. Smith was awed by the advanced technology Hughes had developed, and decided General Motors should acquire the company.

Ross disagreed. He thought GM should concentrate on building cars that Americans wanted to buy. At Board of Directors meetings, he listed consumer problems with GM cars: engines that leaked radiator coolant into the oil, leaky transmissions that fell apart, unattractive body styles. Ross also argued that Hughes was too dependent on federal contracts, which could easily dry up.

At first, Ross kept his arguments against the Hughes purchase contained inside the upper levels of the company's management. But when he realized he was not going to stop the deal, he began speaking publicly. He did not hide his frustration with Roger Smith and the other directors. "Until we nuke the GM system, we'll never tap the full potential of our people," he said to reporters. When asked about the Board of Directors he said: "The board is like a pet rock, just sitting there. It's a joke. Is the board a rubber stamp for Roger [Smith]? No. We'd have to upgrade it to be a rubber stamp."

Then Ross got personal. "He [Smith] is the basic problem. He's emotionally unstable."

From this point there was no turning back. Ross's attacks on GM management were unprecedented in the higher echelons of big business. Either Ross or Smith would have to leave.

Ross knew he would be the one who left. Smith was

supported by the Board of Directors. But he did not go without a fight. Ross may have lost the battle within the company, but he won it among the public. Smith's prestige never recovered.

Smith's reputation suffered more as GM continued to lose money. While Smith was reacting to the bad financial news, Ross attacked executive privileges at the company. "I'd get rid of the executive dining rooms. I would urge the senior executives to locate their offices where real people are doing real work." He also said executive pay should be determined by how successful the company was at beating the competition.

Smith decided he did not care how much it cost to get rid of Ross. He offered Perot $742.8 million for his twelve million shares of stock, almost double what it was then selling for on the market. Ross accepted the deal.

Ross had one final poke at Smith. He announced to the press he would place his check into an escrow account for fifteen days, during which time he could not touch it. He should not be given three-quarters of a billion dollars just to make him go away, he said, when GM had recently laid off over 30,000 workers. It was not a wise use of the shareholder's money. He promised to give it back, and return to his position, when the Board of Directors "regains its senses." Ross knew Smith had no intention of changing his mind. He was making a final point. In fifteen days, Ross picked up his check.

The EDS-GM experiment had failed, but Ross was more famous than ever. The major newspapers and television networks covered the dispute. Books were written about what went wrong. Ross had taken on the company that symbolized the economic greatness of twentieth century America. A common expression during the auto giant's great years was that what was good for GM was good for the nation. Now Ross had accused the great company of being a bloated example of everything wrong with American business. While his other adventures had revealed his boldness and willingness to take risks, his fight with GM showed he was seriously concerned about what was wrong with America. Ross was no longer merely the colorful billionaire from Texas. He was a major American figure.

However, Ross's critics felt he had revealed his own faults as well. His impatience, inability to compromise, habit of ridiculing those who did not agree with him, and tendency to play to the media, may have undercut Ross's effort to correct the problems he wanted solved.

However one felt about Ross Perot, it was obvious he was not easily ignored. After taking his buyout money and returning to Texas, Ross joked that he had tried to take a message to GM that the company needed to change, but that they had "shot the messenger." Soon Ross would take his message to the entire country.

RELUCTANT CANDIDATE

Even during Ross's GM experience he continued his other public activities. While many of the problems he spoke out about, like drug abuse and the poor quality of public education, could not be corrected easily, Ross also continued his more localized charitable works. This way he could see the results quickly.

Ross had an opportunity to purchase an original copy of the Magna Carta, a medieval document the nobles of England had forced King John, famous as the evil King in the Robin Hood legends, to sign in 1215. The Magna Carta is one of the first documents to set out individual liberty as a human right. When Ross heard one of the four original copies of the historic document was available for purchase, he wrote out a check for $1.5 million, and later donated the document to the National Archives.

Over the years, Ross has often given money to causes, or individuals, he thought deserving. When his daughter Suzanne discovered that New York City was closing its mounted police patrol because of lack of money, Ross sent sixteen Tennessee Walkers, equipped with saddles and tack, to keep the unit working.

As requests for contributions increased, Ross established the Perot Foundation. He placed his sister Bette, a former school principal, in charge. The Perot Foundation has given money to inner city schools, to food banks that distribute food to the poor and homeless, and to many other worthwhile charities. Ross is especially concerned with helping children. "The greatest legacy we can leave our children is to develop their intellects fully," Ross has said. His own children are not expecting a giant inheritance, however. He has taught them to value learning the skills necessary to be successful on their own.

During his busy career, the five Perot children had grown up. Ross did not neglect them as he pursued success. He has always held family as his highest priority, and made certain he had plenty of time to spend with them.

***

After leaving GM, Ross quickly started another data processing company, Perot Systems, in June of 1988, which was established as a direct competitor to EDS. Many at GM cried foul, and accused Ross of failing to live up to the terms of the agreement he had signed when he left GM. When he began hiring EDS employees for his new company, GM sued Ross and Perot Systems in the Federal Courts. The results of the court suit were somewhat muddied, but Perot Systems continued to recruit EDS employees.

Despite his victory, Ross's friends could easily see that Perot Systems did not really hold his interest. It just was not the same as in the early days of EDS. True, the data processing field was much more competitive than it had been in the early 1960s, but Ross's enthusiasm for his new company was not hampered by the fierce competition. He had already built one huge company and made more money than most people ever dream of making. Ross simply needed a new challenge, and he progressively turned to the public arena.

Ross was now a folk hero to many Americans. He had been active in many public policy issues, both in Texas and nationally. His exploits as an entrepreneur, his well publicized spat with GM, his work on the POW issue, and the dramatic Iran rescue, had put him in the public eye as a slightly eccentric but capable and formidable patriot. Ross often spoke out on public issues, and he became a popular guest on television talk shows, where he would dispense his brand of common sense on a variety of topics.

In 1990, When Saddam Hussein, dictator of Iraq in the Middle East, moved part of his army across the border and took over the oil-rich but militarily weak county of Kuwait, the United States, along with United Nations forces, sent a huge number of soldiers into the area to keep Saddam from invading Saudi Arabia, and to try to convince him to remove his troops from Kuwait. After diplomatic efforts and an economic boycott had failed, a massive military attack dubbed Desert Storm was launched. The greatest number of troops were from the U.S. Popular support in this country for the operation was highly favorable, though some critics thought Desert Storm was a mistake.

Surprisingly to some, Perot was not in favor of the military intervention, and he was a strong critic of the Bush Administration, which he felt had bungled the affair by earlier providing political and military support to Saddam

Hussein. As he said later, during a speech in November of 1991: "War is great young people getting killed, getting pieces of their bodies blown away. War is the last resort, and if and when we do go to war, we must commit the nation and then commit the troops. Never again should we get into a Vietnam situation where we send men and women off to fight and die."

As the 1992 national elections approached, Perot was asked more and more often why he did not run for president. Although George Bush had been immensely popular as a war leader, now that the Iraqi threat was vanquished people were once again worried about the economy. The nation had been suffering a prolonged recession—or downturn in the business cycle—with increased unemployment and the failure, or downsizing, of many of America's largest businesses. Many Americans began to feel that George Bush was not doing enough to help the economy; his strategy seemed to be simply to wait out the hard times. The Democrats had numerous candidates wanting to be their party's nominee, but at this time none were seen as a threat to Bush.

The pressure on Perot to run for president increased. In

1987, after he spoke before the National Governor's Association, the chairman of that group suggested Perot should try for the White House. The chairman was the then-Governor of Arkansas, Bill Clinton.

With this perceived vacuum of leadership, more people, many of whom were experienced in political campaigns, began to suggest that Ross make the effort. He had always fended off these suggestions, saying he was "temperamentally unsuited" for public office. Ross had always felt that the slow-moving, compromising nature of government would be at odds with his "let's get it done now" attitude, and his reluctance to compromise on, an issue when he believed he was right. His experience at GM had done nothing to dispel this personal insight, and he usually dismissed the suggestions with a smile, or by saying that he would be a "square peg in a round hole" in government.

In February of 1992, Ross went to Nashville, Tennessee, to be the guest on a radio show and to deliver a speech to local civic and business leaders. After the talk, a reporter asked him if there were any circumstances in which he might run for president. This time, Ross gave a somewhat different answer. While insisting he was "not interested" in public office, he went on to say that, if the public was willing to register him as a candidate in all 50 states, he would run as an independent candidate.

This comment delighted the growing group of Americans, mostly businessmen and former military officers, who had been pushing Ross to run for president. They immediately began meeting, looking for a way to push Ross further toward committing to the race.

But Ross, as usual, was one step ahead of them. On February 20, 1992, Ross appeared as a guest on the popular *Larry King Show.* Larry King had earlier been tipped off that Ross had made comments suggesting he might be interested in running, and was determined that Ross would announce on his show. Whether Ross had already planned to make his stunning announcement is something only he knows.

In response to Larry's questions, Ross said that he had been asked by thousands of Americans to run for president as an Independent, someone not affiliated with either the Democratic or Republican parties. After saying he had heard, and had understood their requests, Ross promised to run for president if his supporters met one huge requirement. They must organize petition drives in every state, and gather enough signatures to get his name on the ballot in all fifty.

Toward the end of the show Ross spoke directly into the camera: "Now recognize, you're listening to a guy that doesn't want to do this. But if you, the people, will on your own, put my name on the ballot of all fifty states . . . I think I can promise you're going to see a world-class campaign." He concluded by saying "Now then, God bless you all who have written me and called me. The shoe is on the other foot." Ross meant that it was now up to the people who had been begging him to run to prove they were serious.

When the show was over, Ross went back to his hotel to a confused Margot, who had not known her husband was going to declare himself a presidential candidate. Ross imagined nothing more would come of his announcement. But it was only a few minutes before an unseen supporter pushed a five dollar bill under the Perot's suite door—a campaign contribution. The race had begun.

The entire country was shocked by what happened next. Almost immediately, petition drives sprang up in every state. Lawyers with the skills to understand the complex election laws of each state donated their time; accountants and other professionals began collecting the five dollars per participant that Ross had requested from the volunteers, and thousands of other Americans devoted time to collecting names on petitions required to put Perot on the ballot as an independent candidate.

The campaign that started as a seemingly reluctant offer on a talk show was to turn into a campaign very different from any presidential bid of the past, and one which has changed the entire face of electoral politics in the U.S. First, Perot understood that, with the advent of cable television and instant satellite communications, the old method of traveling non-stop from one state to another shaking hands and giving speeches was obsolete. For example, when his campaign began at a rally in Orlando, Florida, the event was broadcast simultaneously to crowds of supporters gathered in five other states.

This mass media approach could be compared to a concert pianist who, instead of traveling from city to city giving performances for small audiences, gives televised concerts which are heard by millions at one time. Ross also very early on bypassed most of the question-and-answer

Ross makes a point during a taping of the *Donahue* show in March, 1992. Perot has consistently used the talk-show format to reach large audiences. (AP/Wide World Photos)

Perot announces his departure from the political arena at a news conference in Dallas on July 17, 1992. He would re-enter the presidential race on October 1. (AP/Wide World Photos)

issue-oriented shows such as *Face the Nation* and *Meet the Press*, where journalists ask questions and the guest responds. Instead, he preferred talk show forums such as *Donahue* and NBC's *Today* show. Here, he had more time and freedom to concentrate on his message, and to answer questions from a studio audience and from telephone call-in viewers all over the country. This "going to the people" style showed Ross at his best. Though it was not long before both Democratic nominee Bill Clinton and George Bush began to use the talk show format, neither competitor could match Perot's earthy and direct style.

Ross zeroed in on two of the main issues which troubled voters in 1992, and on which the election would hinge. The first was the mounting national debt (money borrowed by the government to run the country). Though all candidates had a plan to lower the debt, Ross felt that it should be reduced quickly, and suggested a combination of higher income taxes, reduced benefits for high income taxpayers, and a large tax on gasoline sales, as the best way solve the the problem.

The second major point was revitalizing the nation's

economy, particularly the manufacturing sector. Perot proposed to accomplish this partly by protecting certain industries from foreign competition by imposing tariffs (a form of import tax) on manufactured goods imported from other countries. Within weeks, Ross was beginning to qualify for state ballots, and popularity polls showed him leading both President Bush and Bill Clinton.

But with political popularity comes close scrutiny, as well as attacks from political opponents. The national media started pursuing stories that cast Ross in an unfavorable light, much as they had Bill Clinton earlier in the campaign. For example, stories of Ross's supposed penchant for hiring private investigators to inspect the private lives of his employees and of business competitors, began appearing in newspaper articles and on radio and television news shows, and jokes about "Inspector Perot" spiced the monologues of late night comedians. There were other stories questioning the dealings of Ross and Ross Jr. with a real estate development near the new Dallas airport.

Following close behind the media scrutiny were the political attacks. When an unverified story appeared that Ross had had George Bush's children investigated, the

President told a television interviewer that he was astounded and hurt. "Leave my children out of it," he said. Vice-President Dan Quayle called Ross "a temperamental tycoon with a contempt for the Constitution."

Many of Ross's intimates remember he was taken aback by the intensity of a presidential campaign, and was soon very concerned about its effect on his children. Ross, who has always been somewhat thin-skinned, bristled at the attacks and charges, and began to wonder out loud if he had made a mistake by entering the race.

Things were not perfect inside the campaign, either. Not surprisingly, the momentum of Ross's popularity became more than his amateur supporters could control. Squabbles over leadership and finances began to plague the individual state campaign offices. Perot, who had entered the race promising he would not turn it over to "professional handlers" who would "diaper and burp me every night before I go to bed," soon realized he needed help from people who knew how to run a nationwide campaign. In order to maintain a bi-partisan spirit, Ross decided to hire two political professionals from different parties, Democrat Hamilton Jordan, a former aide to Jimmy Carter, and Ed

Rollins, who had managed Ronald Reagan's 1984 reelection campaign.

The two professionals, however, soon discovered that Ross had no intention of turning the campaign over to them. They grew increasingly frustrated as Ross rejected most of their suggestions. Perot was particularly hesitant to spend the amount of money, almost $250 million, he was told it would take to have a chance to win the election. He argued against paying for television commercials, for example, because he could always go on the *Larry King Show*, or other free media, to get his message out. Quickly, much as during the GM merger, tension developed between Ross's long-time employees and the new political consultants.

As the Democratic National Convention began in New York City, in July 1992, Ed Rollins suddenly announced he was leaving the Perot campaign. Although he restrained his comments about how the campaign had been developing during his departure announcement, Rollins was clearly angry with Ross, and later made several disparaging comments. The internal turmoil in the Perot camp, plus the media scrutiny and political attacks from George Bush and his aides, were taking their toll on Ross's popularity.

Then, in a move that once again was startling and unprecedented in American politics, Perot quit the race. On July 15, 1992, the last day of the Democratic National Convention, which had successfully showcased Bill Clinton in a favorable light, Ross called a news conference and announced he would no longer be a candidate for president. Many in the stunned audience, and around the country, were unconvinced by the reason given for his sudden withdrawal: "Now that the Democratic Party has revitalized itself, I have concluded we cannot win," Perot said. He expressed concern that his continued participation in the race would force the selection of president into the House of Representatives, and that such a result would "be disruptive to the country." After announcing his stunning message, Perot turned and walked abruptly off the stage without taking reporter's questions.

In mentioning the House of Representatives, Ross was referring to the procedure that would take place if no candidate won a majority of the available electoral vote. The Constitution provided in that case for the U.S. House of Representatives to then select a president, with each state having one vote.

Although Ross refused to elaborate on his reasons for pulling out, the announcement shocked the country, and instantly changed the dynamics of the presidential campaign. Within three days of Ross's announcement, Bill Clinton jumped thirty points in the polls, and began the final sprint that eventually led him to the White House.

Despite Perot's departure from the race, the petition drives went on, and Ross continued to fund the volunteer groups. There are some who know Ross personally who believe he never intended to stay out of the race. Others think that the negative press he received for dropping out, especially a major news magazine that pictured a thumb size Ross with the single word "Quitter" on its cover, hurt his pride so deeply that he had no choice but to reenter. Stories quickly began circulating throughout the summer and into the autumn that Ross again was going to be a candidate.

On September 22, Perot, in another television interview, admitted he had "made a mistake" in dropping out. He continued on to say that the major candidates, George Bush and Bill Clinton, were not addressing the important issues of the campaign. People familiar with Ross knew then that he was indicating he would reenter the race.

On October 1, 1992, after meeting with delegations from both the Bush and Clinton campaigns, Ross announced that he was back in the running. Appearing on the stage with Perot and Margot was Admiral James Stockdale, who had been held prisoner for seven years during the Vietnam War, and would serve as Ross's running mate. However, his popularity was less than 10% in most polls. Most analysts thought he would not have a significant impact on the race.

But the experts were not counting on the force of the Perot personality. Ross reentered the campaign with enough time to participate in the three scheduled televised debates. Although most pundits agree that Bill Clinton decisively won the second debate, held in Richmond, Virginia, on October 19, Ross was probably the biggest surprise. With his Texas twang and gift for pithy one-liners, Ross won over thousands of viewers who were worried about his seemingly erratic behavior. He began to climb yet again in the polls.

The next strategy of Ross's campaign also defied the professionals, and won Ross respect even from his most vocal critics. Instead of investing in dozens of thirty and sixty-second commercials, Ross purchased, with his own

Ross with pointer stick and one of his famous graphs during a television "commercial" during the presidential campaign in October 1992. (AP/ Wide World Photos)

Perot greets candidates Bill Clinton and George Bush before their debate in East Lansing, Michigan, late in the 1992 presidential campaign. (AP/ Wide World Photos)

money, thirty-minute blocks of time on the major networks during primetime. On these programs Ross, armed only with a stack of charts and a metal pointer, explained his views on the nation's most critical problems—the national debt and the need for political reform. He sat behind a table, and spoke directly into the camera. There was no glitz or inspirational theme music. One political advisor described the shows as "castor oil." However, the paid programs were immensely popular. Millions of people, even many who were not going to vote for Ross, watched them and expressed gratitude that a political candidate had attempted to explain the real problems facing the country instead of attempting to sway their emotions with patriotic footage or simply attack their opponents. Although Ross, especially in the last two weeks of the race, did not hesitate to attack his opponents, many think his fact-filled programs are his greatest contribution to American politics.

Because of his television strategy, and his performance in the debates, Ross began moving back up in the popularity polls. Although he never approached the level of support necessary to win the election, his ability to come back into a campaign he had so suddenly departed from, and to regain strength so quickly, was astounding. But, when Ross went onto the popular CBS news magazine *60 Minutes* and announced that the reason he had withdrawn from the race in July was because the Bush "dirty tricks people" had threatened to disrupt his daughter's August wedding, and had doctored photographs in a manner that would embarrass her, many of the old questions about Perot's judgment again came to the forefront. The comments directly conflicted with the reasons for dropping out he had given earlier, and now the media began asking for proof that Perot's charges were true. When Ross could not produce convincing evidence of his charges, the news coverage turned negative once again, and Ross's ascent in the polls stalled.

On election day, however, Ross won 19% of the popular vote, more than any third party candidate had won since Theodore Roosevelt in 1912. Although he had certainly run the most unusual presidential campaign in American history, and had seemed to toy with political self-destruction, Ross had seized the imaginations of millions of Americans, and had guaranteed that he would have an impact on the immediate political future of the United States.

CITIZEN PEROT

What is the more personal side of Ross Perot, this billionaire who has so captivated the imaginations of millions of Americans? Certainly, there is no question that Ross lives in luxury, though in some respects he is still the small town boy who delivered newspapers on horseback.

Ross has never scrimped when it has come to the comfort and safety of his family. The Perots have four homes. The first, the main residence, is located in North Dallas on 20 acres of carefully landscaped grounds. The house is a spacious red brick mansion with wide, columned entrances. The house and grounds contain a bowling alley, a gymnasium with basketball court which the Perots convert to a dance floor for large formal gatherings, a swimming pool, tennis courts, and riding stables. The safety of his family is of the greatest importance to Ross, and the estate is surrounded by a high wall. Armed security guards, mostly off-duty Dallas policemen, roam the grounds.

The Perots' favorite vacation home is a 12-acre estate on Lake Texoma, a two-hour drive north of Dallas. For weekend skiing, the family enjoys a chalet located in Vail, Colorado, an exclusive resort town frequented by movie stars and society types. The most luxurious vacation retreat is *Caliban*, located in Tucker's Town, Bermuda, which Ross purchased in 1985. The estate, built in the days of the British crown colony, is perched high on a rocky cliff overlooking the ocean.

When unwinding, Perot prefers hobbies and sports that include speed and movement. He enjoys skiing and is said to be talented at the sport. At Lake Texoma, and in Bermuda, he enjoys operating his ocean-going speedboats, known as Cigarette boats because of their long slender shape. He is also fond of Jet Skis and wind surfing. But the most impressive vehicle in the Perot fleet is *Chateau Margaux*, a 51-foot yacht.

There seems to be quite a difference in what Ross spends for his family and what he spends for himself personally.

Though he enjoys lavishing Margot with jewelry, Ross drives around Dallas in a second-hand Oldsmobile. His business suits are conservatively cut and bought off the rack. His close cropped-hair is trimmed once a week at a local barber shop. Though he occasionally dines out with his family and friends at expensive restaurants, Perot's favorite place for lunch is Dickey's Barbecue Pit, a cafeteria style eatery serving down-home favorites, where he is almost certainly the only billionaire in sight.

As reported by several local papers, Ross can often be found at a Home Depot store near his residence, searching for hardware to make repairs or home improvements to his mansion.

Margot Perot says her "first priority" has always been "the family and creating a happy home life for Ross." And certainly the durable Perot marriage is also stable and happy. Margot, who is three years younger than Ross, is given much of the credit by her husband for raising a happy family. He says Margot is a "world class mother," responsible for the smooth functioning of the family while much of his energy had to be devoted to business. "Five out of my five kids are too good to be true, thanks to their mother."

Margot is an active person, keeping fit with long walks. She also attends an occasional aerobics class, plays tennis and skis when the family is at their Vail, Colorado, chalet. But most of her time is taken up with a variety of charity and volunteer causes. She is a board member of the Dallas Salvation Army, and during holidays mends donated toys for their Christmas giving programs. A Presbyterian with strong church ties, she is also on the board of the Presbyterian Hospital of Dallas (to which the family recently endowed a women's and children's center). Margot is a supporter of Planned Parenthood, and cares deeply about the problems of child abuse, family violence, and other issues of special concern to women and children. Margot also finds time to devote to the United Way, the Texas Commission on the Arts, and the Dallas Museum of Art.

Katherine, the youngest Perot, is a recent graduate of the University of North Carolina at Chapel Hill. Carolyn, the next youngest, lives not too far from the family home in Dallas. Suzanne is married to a stockbroker and has worked for the celebrated auction house, Christie's, in New York City. Nancy, the oldest daughter, is also married and works as a specialist in venture capital for an affiliated company of Perot Systems. Ross Jr., now in his mid-thirties, handles many of the real estate holdings and developments of The Perot Group. In September, 1982, Ross Jr. accomplished a personal long-time goal by making a solitary round-the-world trip in a single-engine Bell Ranger helicopter.

Some people have a hard time understanding Ross Perot. Many of the things he does seem to be contradictory or paradoxical. He does not fit easily into any category, such as Democrat or Republican, Liberal or Conservative. A brillant businessman, who has always claimed to believe in free trade, and competition between companies, Ross has nevertheless come out against the North American Free Trade Agreement (NAFTA). NAFTA would remove tariffs and other trade barriers between the United States, Canada and Mexico. NAFTA's supporters believe this opening of markets would create the largest trading block in the world, and open greater markets for American manufacturers to sell their products. NAFTA's opponents are afraid the treaty would make it easier for American companies to move their manufacturing and service facilities to Mexico, where labor is cheap and abundant, and where environmental regulations are lax. Perot had said the agreement would create a "giant sucking sound" of jobs being taken away from American workers and given to the exploited workers of Mexico. He believes that this would not only harm America, but also would not help Mexican workers because the increased revenues would not raise the living standards of the average wage earner.

There is no doubt that Perot can be a charismatic leader who inspires loyalty, and who expects—and usually gets—excellence from the people under him. However, some political analysts think that Perot can be the most help and do the most good for the country right where he is, as an outside motivator and organizer of private citizens, directing his energy toward one issue at a time. His access to popular talk shows, and his obvious audience appeal, almost guarantee that his views will continue to gain wide publicity and will force those in public office to take him seriously. His organization, United We Stand, America, with its growing, motivated membership, cannot be ignored by national and state leaders. It is large enough that, with or without direction from Perot, its membership can decide a close congressional or gubernatorial election.

It appears that Ross Perot will be an important public figure in the United States in the future. Presidential bids and thorny political issues aside, something about Perot speaks to the deep and heartfelt needs and aspirations of many Americans, rich or poor, black or white. This is a time when many people are cynical about government, and half-believe that the goodness and strength of America is becoming a thing of the past. Ross Perot, in many of the things he says, and more importantly, in many of the things he does, stands as a powerful personal repudiation to the cynics and naysayers. It is this quality of unabashed (some would say naive) patriotism and optimisim that most endears him to his supporters.

Another characteristic of Ross is his frankness, and his ability to summarize, in simple language, many Americans' own frustrations with their government. His willingness to express things other politicians avoid saying is refreshing in an era of highly paid political consultants and politics by popularity polls. As he once said: "If voters don't have a stomach for me, they can get one of those blow-dried guys."

Beyond anything else, Perot is most definitely not a man surrounded by public relations advisors and handlers. He is, for lack of a better word, real. He says what he believes to be true, and then, sometimes at maximum personal and political risk, acts on his beliefs. And, whether they agree with Perot or not, many of his fellow citizens appreciate and admire these qualities.

Perot has also created doubts about himself in the minds of many voters. His erratic behavior during the 1992 campaign left some wondering whether he has the personal steadiness necessary to be the nation's leader. Doubts are also created by the fact that Ross has performed best in endeavors over which he had total control. He has yet to show the capacity to work well within organizations resistant to the control of a single individual, such as the immense and complicated U. S. government.

However, Ross Perot has clearly developed a solid base of support, and will doubtless continue to play an important role in American public life. And, although it is impossible to predict what he will do in the future, one thing is certain. Ross Perot will continue to fascinate.

CHRONOLOGY

1930   Born in Texarkana, Texas.

1949-1953   Attends U. S. Naval Academy.

1953-1957   Serves in U. S. Navy.

1956   Marries Margot Birmingham.

1957-1962   Works for International Business Machines (IBM).

1962   Starts Electronic Data Systems (EDS).

1969   Takes EDS public, becomes a billionaire.

1969-1973   Works to free American POWs held in North Vietnam.

1979   Frees EDS employees held hostage in Iran.

1984   Sells EDS to General Motors (GM). Joins GM Board of Directors.

1986   Leaves GM.

1988   Begins Perot Systems.

1992   Runs for President of the United States. Starts United We Stand, America.

FOR FURTHER READING

Chiu, Tony: *Ross Perot: In His Own Words*, Warner Books: New York, 1992.

Follett, Ken: *On Wings Of Eagles*, W. W. Morrow: New York, 1983.

Germond, Jack and Jules Witcover: *Mad As Hell: Revolt At The Ballot Box, 1992*, Warner Books: New York, 1993.

Gross, Ken: *Ross Perot: The Man Behind The Myth*, Random House: New York, 1992.

Mason, Todd: *Perot: An Unauthorized Biography*, Business One Irwin, Homewood, Illinois, 1990.

Index

religion, 18
sells EDS, 96
starts Perot Systems, 107
takes EDS public, 53-54
use of mass media, 113-115,
118, 121-123
Perot, Katherine, 43, 128
Perot, Lulu May Ray, 11, 16, 18,
31
Perot, Margot Birmingham, 27-
28, 30-33, 36-37, 43-45, 91-92,
99, 112, 121, 127-128
Perot, Nancy, 43, 92, 128
Perot, Ross Jr., 43, 90-92, 116,
127
Perot, Suzanne, 43, 91, 106, 128
Perot Systems, 107, 129
Port Said, 31
Prisoners of War (POWs), 59-68

Qasr Prison, 79-80
Quayle, Dan, 117
Quonset Naval Station, 33

Ray, Henry, 20-21
Readers Digest, 44
Reagan, Nancy, 89
Red River, 15
Reidlinger, Ken, 97
Rollins, Ed, 118

Salomon Brothers, 93
Saturday Evening Post, 15
Saudi Arabia, 108
SAVAK, 70, 73
Schuman, Sam, 18
Shah Pahlevi, 70, 72-75

Shiite Muslims, 73
Simons, Colonel Arthur D., 68,
77-79, 83
Singapore, 29
Smith, Roger, 94-103
Son Tay Prison, 68
Son Tay Raiders, 68
Stockdale, Admiral James, 121

Teheran, 71-72, 75, 77-80
Texarkana Gazette, 13-14
Texarkana Junior College, 21-23,
26
Today, 115
Tucker's Town, Bermuda, 126
Turkey, 78

United We Stand, America, 130
U. S. Embassy (Teheran), 82
U. S. House of Representatives,
119
U. S. Naval Academy, 21, 25-28
U. S. State Department, 75-76
USS Leyte, 32-35
USS Sigourney, 29-32

Vail, Colorado, 126, 128
Vietnam War, 57-68

Watson, Thomas, 37
Wayne, John, 68
White, Mark, 85
Wickford, Rhode Island, 33